T0194986

HEBREWS
AND
JAMES

Gerald McDaniel

WESTBOW
P R E S S®
A DIVISION OF THOMAS NELSON
& ZONDERVAN

This book is a work of non-fiction. Unless otherwise noted, the author
and the publisher make no explicit guarantees as to the accuracy of
the information contained in this book and in some cases, names
of people and places have been altered to protect their privacy.

WestBow Press books may be ordered through booksellers or by contacting:

WestBow Press
A Division of Thomas Nelson & Zondervan
1663 Liberty Drive
Bloomington, IN 47403
www.westbowpress.com
1 (866) 928-1240

Because of the dynamic nature of the Internet, any web addresses or
links contained in this book may have changed since publication and
may no longer be valid. The views expressed in this work are solely those
of the author and do not necessarily reflect the views of the publisher,
and the publisher hereby disclaims any responsibility for them.

Any people depicted in stock imagery provided by Getty Images are models,
and such images are being used for illustrative purposes only.
Certain stock imagery © Getty Images.

Scripture taken from the King James Version of the Bible.

ISBN: 978-1-9736-9162-4 (sc)
ISBN: 978-1-9736-9163-1 (e)

Print information available on the last page.

WestBow Press rev. date: 05/07/2020

A Personal Letter to
my Grandchildren

I would like to share, first of all, a partial personal testimony out of my own life. Many years ago, as a small young boy I was extremely shy and very much an introvert. I would do most anything to avoid standing up in front of people and speaking especially in front of a school class. Even in sports on the basketball court the intimidation of the crowd no matter how large or small would greatly hinder me from playing basketball as well as I was able.

I had a dear grandmother who was a precious Christian lady. When she would come to stay with our family from time to time, she would always call me her little preacher boy. I hated it because even though I was lost at the time I knew that it would mean getting up in front of people. Needless to say, I regretted it every time grandmother came around.

At the age of 20 years old I trusted Christ as my personal Savior. At the age of 21 years old, strange as it may seem, God called me to preach. My grandmother was right.

Having said this I am convinced just like grandmother was that I will have a grandchild whether born or adopted, girl or boy that God will call to take the books that I have written and learn them and be able to understand them and teach from them and use them in their ministry that God has for them.

Be advised, you will run into many that do not agree with the teachings in these books. You will probably have family that will not agree with the teachings in these books. Either way as a little girl in writing or teaching ladies or as a little boy in writing or teaching and preaching, I am convinced God will raise up one of my grandchildren to a ministry that these books will be greatly used.

Please understand at the time of this writing, there have been 4 books published and 2 written yet to be published with more to come. At this time, you may not even be born yet or adopted yet. Even though all my grandchildren are welcome to these books and will have access to these books, I am convinced as much as I am alive that God will raise up one of you with a special ministry directly related to these books.

If I live long enough, I will be able to witness this taking place, firsthand. My grandmother died before she was able to hear me preach. Please be aware that I am not writing these books as a hobby neither are they written to make money. It is a God called ministry. There will be many more books written and all my grandchildren will have access to them if that is their desire. I want to reassure you of course that I love all my grandchildren.

There will be one with a special calling. May God bless you little one and I am praying for you now even if you have not been born or adopted yet. Granddaddy loves you very much and is excited about what God will do in your life.

This letter will be published with the future books to make sure you get a copy of this letter.

Contents

1

The Plan of Salvation

Let's go through **4 H's. Honesty, Humility, Helpless, and Hope**

H #1) *You must be **HONEST** enough to admit you have sinned and broken God's commands. Understand in doing so this puts you in very great danger!*

Romans 3:10 "there is none righteous, no not one."

Romans 3:23 "…all have sinned…"

I John 1:8 "if we say that we have no sin, we deceive ourselves, and the truth is not in us."

H #2) *You must be **HUMBLE** enough to admit you deserve Hell when you die.*

One sin disqualifies us from Heaven, and we have all sinned more than once.

Romans 6:23 "For the wages of sin [is] death"

Revelation 21:8 "But the fearful, and unbelieving, and the abominable, and murderers, and whoremongers, and sorcerers, and idolaters, and all liars, shall have their part in the lake which burneth with fire and brimstone: which is the second death."

H **#3)** *You must understand you are **HELPLESS** when it comes to you saving yourself from going to Hell when you die. There is nothing you can do to pay for your own sin.*

Ephesians 2:8-9 For by grace are ye saved through faith; and that not of yourselves: it is the gift of God: not of works, lest any man should boast.

Titus 3:5 Not by works of righteousness which we have done, but according to his mercy he saved us, by the washing of regeneration, and renewing of the Holy Ghost;

Galatians 2:16 Knowing that a man is not justified by the works of the law, but by the faith of Jesus Christ, even we have believed in Jesus Christ, that we might be justified by the faith of Christ, and not by the works of the law: for by the works of the law shall no flesh be justified.

Understand when I say HELPLESS it means you cannot surrender your life to Christ for salvation. You have no life to surrender. You are dead in trespasses and sins. You cannot yet make Jesus the Lord of your life because you have no life. Jesus will not be Lord of your life until He is Savior of your soul. You cannot turn from your sins because you are dead in your sins. You must see yourself HELPLESS at the Mercy of God. Now you are ready for H # 4.

H   #4)   *You are helpless but not hopeless. Your **HOPE** must be in Jesus, God's Son and what he has done for you on the cross when He died there. Jesus is the only one that paid for your sins when he died on the cross. He was buried and arose again. You must ask Jesus to be your personal Savior and ask Jesus to save you from Hell. If you are depending on church membership to save you, that means you are not depending on Jesus to save you. If you are depending on the good deeds you do to save you, that means you are not depending on Jesus to save you. If you are depending on baptism to save you, that means you are not depending on Jesus to save you. It must be Jesus and what Jesus did for you on the cross that you are depending on to save you. Nothing else can go with this. Jesus is the only one who paid for your sins on the cross so Jesus is the only one who can save you.*

Romans 5:8 But God commendeth his love toward us, in that, while we were yet sinners, Christ died for us.

I Peter 3:18 For Christ also hath once suffered for sins, the just for the unjust, that he might bring us to God, being put to death in the flesh but quickened by the Spirit.

Hebrews 10:12 But this man (JESUS) after he hath offered one sacrifice for sins for ever, sat down on the right hand of God.

John 14:6 Jesus saith unto him, I am the way, the truth, and the life: no man cometh unto the Father, but by me.

Acts 4:12 Neither is there salvation in any other: for there is none other name under heaven given among men, whereby we must be saved.

John 3:16 For God so loved the world, that he gave his only begotten Son, that whosoever believeth in him should not perish, but have everlasting life.

Ask Jesus to save you before it is too late:

Romans 10:13 For whosoever shall call upon the name of the Lord shall be saved.

2

Introduction to Hebrews

First allow me to give an explanation of what I call a "word study sentence" that will appear several times in this book. Most software Bible programs can produce these "word study sentences" at the stroke of a few keys. Note the following example:

Note: The word "**study**" in II Tim. 2:15 #4704 (11x) (endeavour-3; do diligence-2; be diligent-2; give diligence; be forward; **labour**; study)

You will need two books to aid in producing the "Word Study Sentence."

1) The Strong's Concordance for the KJV Bible
2) The New Strong's Expanded Dictionary of Bible Words

Allow me to explain each part of the word study sentence. "Study" is the word in question that is being looked up. The next part is the Strong's number for that word which represents the Greek word for the word "study" which is #4704. It is Greek because the word in question is in the New Testament. Simply look up the word "study" in the Strong's just like you would look up a word in a dictionary. After finding the word "study" in the Strong's, you can see below the word and to the left many New Testament references and then the reference, II Timothy 2:15. To the right on the same line with the verse you can see the Strong's number #4704. With "The New Strong's Expanded Dictionary of Bible Words" you can produce the following information as well as most Bible software programs. The next part in the word study sentence is the number followed by an "x" which is how many times that (#4704) appears in the New Testament. It appears 11 times. Next are the different ways the (#4704) are translated in the King James Bible followed by the number of times each word appears in the New Testament. These different English translations because of the preservation of both the English and Greek produce synonyms and definitions for the word "STUDY." There is not only computer software available to produce this word study sentence, but also other hard copy books out that can give you the same information.

Now, back to the study on the "Book of Hebrews."

True to its label is the fact that the "Book of Hebrews" was written first to the Jews and then obviously to all believers. Hebrews has an underlying theme to reach the unbelieving Jews for Christ. Notice the following basic overall perspectives of the book of Hebrews.

1) **Theme to and key word to the Book of Hebrews is the word, "Better" (13 Times) "more excellent" (3 Times).**

   Now notice the following scripture references with the word "better" or the phrase "more excellent."

Better than Angels and More Excellent Name

Hebrews 1:4 *Being made so **much better than the angels**, as he hath by inheritance obtained a **more excellent name** than they.*

Better Things

Hebrews 6:9 *But, beloved, we are persuaded **better things** of you, and things that accompany salvation, though we thus speak.*

Better

Hebrews 7:7 *And without all contradiction the less is blessed of the **better**.*

Better Hope

Hebrews 7:19 *For the law made nothing perfect, but the bringing in of a **better hope** did; by the which we draw nigh unto God.*

Better Testament

Hebrews 7:22 *By so much was Jesus made a surety of a **better testament**.*

More Excellent Ministry & Better Promises & Better Covenant

Hebrews 8:6 *But now hath he obtained a **more excellent ministry**, by how much also he is the mediator of a **better covenant**, which was established upon **better promises**.*

Better Sacrifices

Hebrews 9:23 *It was therefore necessary that the patterns of things in the heavens should be purified with these; but the heavenly things themselves with **better sacrifices** than these.*

Better and Enduring Substance

Hebrews 10:34 *For ye had compassion of me in my bonds, and took joyfully the spoiling of your goods, knowing in yourselves that ye have in heaven a **better and an enduring substance.***

More Excellent Sacrifice

Hebrews 11:4 *By faith Abel offered unto God **a more excellent sacrifice** than Cain, by which he obtained witness that he was righteous, God testifying of his gifts: and by it he being dead yet speaketh.*

Better Country

Hebrews 11:16 *But now they desire a* ***better country****, that is, an heavenly: wherefore God is not ashamed to be called their God: for he hath prepared for them a city.*

Better Resurrection

Hebrews 11:35 *Women received their dead raised to life again: and others were tortured, not accepting deliverance; that they might obtain a* ***better resurrection****:*

Better Thing

Hebrews 11:40 *God having provided some* ***better thing*** *for us, that they without us should not be made perfect.*

Better Things

Hebrews 12:24 *And to Jesus the mediator of the new covenant, and to the blood of sprinkling, that speaketh* ***better things*** *than that of Abel.*

2) **The pattern is Mostly Bible Doctrine: Hebrews deals more with the way we should believe than the way we should live. <u>What you believe defines what and who you are.</u> Learning and believing Bible doctrine stabilizes your life and makes you able to help others.**

Isaiah 33:6 *And <u>**wisdom and knowledge shall be the stability of thy times**</u>, and strength of salvation: the fear of the LORD is his treasure.*

Hosea 4:6 <u>**My people are destroyed for lack of knowledge**</u>: *because thou hast rejected knowledge, I will also reject thee, that thou shalt be no priest to me: seeing thou hast forgotten the law of thy God, I will also forget thy children.*

The Statement of Faith of a church or group must be accurate with the Bible and circulated and understood and believed by the church or group. It is not only a sin to do wrong and not to do right, it is also a sin to believe wrong and not to believe right.

Titus 3:10 *A man that is an <u>**heretick**</u> after the first and second admonition reject;*

Galatians 5:19-21 *Now the works of the flesh are manifest, which are these; Adultery, fornication, uncleanness, lasciviousness,* **20** *Idolatry, witchcraft, hatred, variance, emulations, wrath, strife, seditions, <u>**heresies**</u>,* **21** *Envyings, murders, drunkenness, revellings, and such like: of the which I tell you before, as I have also told you in time past, that they which do such things shall not inherit the kingdom of God.*

If I could afford it, I would put a copy of the Book of Hebrews in the hand of every unbelieving Jew. The entire Book of Hebrews is a wonderful gospel tract to the unbelieving Jew. It answers every question that the Jew might have and reveals the true history of the Jew in the process. This is why there should be no surprise to the fact that the author to the Book of Hebrews is not revealed in the book itself. This author believes that the human author to the Book of Hebrews is Paul, the Apostle.

3

Hebrews Chapter 1

How God Spoke to Mankind through the Ages

Heb 1:1 God, who at sundry times and in divers manners spake in time past unto the fathers **by the prophets,**

Note: God spoke to man in times past by the prophets and now speaks to us through the prophet's writings. In other words, God now speaks to us through the Word of God, the Bible.

Jesus is Son of God
Jesus is Heir of all Things
Jesus Is the Creator

Heb 1:2 Hath in these last days spoken unto us by [his] **Son**, whom he hath appointed <u>heir of all things</u>, <u>by whom also he made the worlds</u>;

Note: Jesus is the spokesman for the Father.

Note: Jesus is appointed heir of all things.

Note: Jesus is the Creator:

> **Colossians 1:16** <u>**For by him were all things created**</u>, *that are in heaven, and that are in earth, visible and invisible, whether they be thrones, or dominions, or principalities, or powers:* <u>**all things were created by him, and for him**</u>*:*

> **John 1:3** <u>**All things were made by him**</u>*; and without him was not any thing made that was made.*

> **Ephesians 3:9** *And to make all men see what is the fellowship of the mystery, which from the beginning of the world hath been hid in* <u>**God, who created all things by Jesus Christ:**</u>

Jesus is the Image of God the Father
Jesus is the Upholder of Creation

Heb 1:3 Who being the brightness of [his] glory, and <u>the express image of his</u> **person #5287**, and **upholding #5342** <u>all things by the word of his power</u>, when <u>he had</u> **by himself** <u>purged our sins</u>, sat down on the right hand of the Majesty on high;

> *Note: "person" [#5287][5x][confidence 2, confident 1, person 1, substance 1]*

(Heb 11:1) Now faith is the **substance #5287** of things hoped for, the evidence of things not seen.

The Person or Substance of our faith is Jesus.

Note: "upholding" #5342 (64x)(bring-34; bear-8; bring forth-5; come-3; reach-2;endure-2; carry; upholding; misc-8)

Note: Jesus is the one who purges all our sins. (One of many reasons why Jesus died) Notice the phrase, "by himself." Our works or deeds have no part in purging our sins. It is Jesus by Himself that purges our sins. Also, Jesus did not need any help.

(John 10:17) Therefore doth my Father love me, because **I lay down my life, that I might take it again. (John 10:18) No man taketh it from me, but I lay it down of myself. I have power to lay it down, and I have power to take it again**. This commandment have I received of my Father.

Note: After Jesus' death on the cross, Jesus is now at the right hand of the Father in heaven.

Jesus is Better Than the Angels
Jesus Has a More Excellent Name

Heb 1:4 Being made so much **better** than the angels, as he hath by inheritance obtained a <u>more excellent name</u> than they.

Note: Jesus is better than the angels because Jesus is the creator of the angels. Jesus has the greatest name.

C.R. **Phil. 2:9** <u>Wherefore God also hath highly exalted</u> <u>him, and</u> **given him a name which Is above every** **name**<u>: 10</u> <u>That at the name of</u> **Jesus** <u>every knee should</u> <u>bow, of things in heaven, and things in earth, and things</u> <u>under the earth;</u> **11** *And that every tongue should confess that Jesus Christ is Lord, to the glory of God the Father.*

Acts 4:12 *Neither is there salvation in any other: for there is none other name under heaven given among men, whereby we must be saved.*

Jesus is the Only Begotten Son of The Father
Jesus is the Son of God

Heb 1:5 For unto which of the angels said he at any time, **Thou art my Son, this day have I begotten thee**? And again, **I will be to him a Father, and he shall be to me a Son**?

Note: **Ps 2:7** *I will declare the decree: the LORD hath said unto me,* **Thou art my Son; this day have I begotten thee.**

2Sam 7:14 <u>**I will be his father, and he shall be my son**</u>. *If he commit iniquity, I will chasten him with the rod of men, and with the stripes of the children of men:*

Jesus is the Son of God

1John 2:23 <u>**Whosoever denieth the Son, the same**</u> <u>**hath not the Father: (but) he that acknowledgeth the**</u> <u>**Son hath the Father also**</u>.

1John 4:15 <u>**Whosoever shall confess that Jesus is the Son of God, God dwelleth in him, and he in God.**</u>

Jesus is the Only Begotten Son

John 3:16 For God so loved the world, that he gave **<u>his only begotten Son</u>**, that whosoever believeth in him should not perish, but have everlasting life.

John 1:14 And the Word was made flesh, and dwelt among us, (and we beheld his glory, the glory as of **<u>the only begotten of the Father</u>**,) full of grace and truth.

John 1:18 No man hath seen God at any time; **<u>the only begotten Son</u>**, which is in the bosom of the Father, he hath declared him.

John 3:18 He that believeth on him is not condemned: but he that believeth not is condemned already, because he hath not believed in the name of **<u>the only begotten Son of God.</u>**

1John 4:9 In this was manifested the love of God toward us, because that God sent **<u>his only begotten Son</u>** into the world, that we might live through him.

God the Father Commands that Jesus should be Worshipped

Heb 1:6 And again, when <u>he bringeth in the **firstbegotten** into the world</u>, he saith, And <u>let all the angels of God worship him</u>.

Note: **Exodus 34:14** <u>For thou shalt worship no other god:</u> <u>for the LORD, whose name is Jealous, is a jealous God:</u>

Revelation 22:8-9 *And I John saw these things, and heard them. And when I had heard and seen, I fell down to worship before the feet of the angel which shewed me these things. 9 Then saith he unto me, See thou do it not: for I am thy fellowservant, and of thy brethren the prophets, and of them which keep the sayings of this book:* **<u>worship God.</u>**

Note: "firstbegotten" #4416 [9x}[firstborn 7, first begotten 2]

C.R. **Colossians 1:15** *Who is the image of the invisible God, the <u>firstborn</u> of every creature:* **16** *For by him were all things created, that are in heaven, and that are in earth, visible and invisible, whether they be thrones, or dominions, or principalities, or powers: all things were created by him, and for him:* **17** *And he is before all things, and by him all things consist.* **18** *And he is the head of the body, the church: who is the beginning, the* **<u>firstborn</u>** *from the dead; that in all things he might have the preeminence.*

Note: C.R. **Ps 97:7** *Confounded be all they that serve graven images, that boast themselves of idols:* **<u>worship</u>** **<u>him</u>***, all ye gods.*

Note: *God commanded the angels of God to worship Jesus. This gives support to the Deity of Christ in that God the Father would command that Jesus should be worshipped. When mankind and idols are forbiddened to be worshipped, God the Father commands us and angels to worship Jesus because Jesus is God the Son.*

The True Nature of Angels

Heb 1:7 And of the angels he saith, Who maketh his angels spirits, and his ministers a flame of fire.

Note: "angels" [32][186x][angel 179, messenger 7]

Note: "angels" [2465][1x]

Luke 20:36 *Neither can they die any more: for they are **equal unto the angels**; and are the children of God, being the children of the resurrection.*

*Note: C.R. **Ps 104:4** Who maketh his angels spirits; his ministers a flaming fire:*

God the Father calls Jesus, God

Heb 1:8 But <u>unto the Son [he saith]</u>, **Thy throne, O God**, [is] forever and ever: a sceptre of righteousness [is] the sceptre of thy kingdom.

Note: "sceptre" [#4464][12x][staves or staff-4; rod-6; scepter-2]

*Note: C.R. v.8-9 - **Ps 45:6** Thy throne, O God, is for ever and ever: the sceptre of thy kingdom is a right sceptre. 7 Thou lovest righteousness, and hatest wickedness: therefore God, thy God, hath anointed thee with the oil of gladness above thy fellows.*

Note: Here God the Father calls Jesus "God". Notice the phrase, 'unto the Son he saith.' The He is God the Father that is speaking.

Jesus Is God the Son

Phil 2:6 *Who**, being in the form of God, thought it not robbery to be equal with God**: 7 But made himself of no reputation, and took upon him the form of a servant, and was made in the likeness of men: **8)** And being found in fashion as a man, he humbled himself, and became obedient unto death, even the death of the cross.**9** Wherefore God also hath highly exalted him, and given him a name which is above every name:*

1Tim 3:16 *And without controversy great is the mystery of godliness:* **God was manifest in the flesh**, *justified in the Spirit, seen of angels, preached unto the Gentiles, believed on in the world, received up into glory.*

John 1:1 *In the beginning was the Word, and the Word was with God, and* **the Word was God.**

1John 5:20 *And we know that the Son of God is come, and hath given us an understanding, that we may know him that is true, and we are in him that is true, even in* **his Son Jesus Christ. This is the true God, and eternal life***.*

Titus 2:13 *Looking for that blessed hope, and the glorious appearing* **of the great God and our Saviour Jesus Christ;**

John 20:28 *And Thomas answered and said unto him,* **_My Lord and my God_**.

Isa 9:6 *For unto us a child is born, unto us a son is given: and the government shall be upon his shoulder: and his name shall be called Wonderful, Counsellor,* **_The mighty God_**, *The everlasting Father, The Prince of Peace.*

Why Jesus was Anointed

Heb 1:9 Thou hast loved righteousness, and hated iniquity; therefore God, [even] thy God, hath anointed thee with the oil of gladness above thy fellows.

Note: The reason given here for Jesus being filled with the Holy Spirit is and would be the same as for us. That is if we will love righteousness and hate sin.

Creator versus Creation

Heb 1:10 And, Thou, Lord, in the beginning hast laid the foundation of the earth; and the heavens are the works of thine hands:

Heb 1:11 They shall perish; but thou remainest; and they all shall wax old as doth a garment;

Note: C.R. for v. 10-12

Ps 102:25 *Of old hast thou laid the foundation of the earth: and the heavens are the work of thy hands.* **26** *They shall perish, but thou shalt endure: yea, all of them shall* *wax old like a garment; as a vesture shalt thou change them, and they shall be changed: 27 But thou art the same, and thy years shall have no end.*

Note: All of creation is getting older and aging but not God.

Heb 1:12 And as a **vesture** shalt thou fold them up, and they shall be changed: but **thou art the same, and thy years shall not fail.**

Note: "vesture" #4018 (2x)(covering – I Cor. 11:15, vesture)

Note: Jesus is forever. (Jesus in His Person is perfect and if Jesus ever changes he would be less than perfect. Even though salvation has and will always be the same, the way God has dealt with mankind down through time has changed.) For a few examples: dietary laws; sabbath day worship; circumcision; sacrificial laws according to the Scriptures, have all been fulfilled and are no longer practiced.

Heb 13:8 *Jesus Christ the same yesterday, and to day, and for ever.*

Jesus versus Angels

Heb 1:13 But to which of the angels said he at any time, Sit on my right hand, until I make thine enemies thy footstool?

Note: C.R. **Ps 110:1** *The LORD said unto my Lord, Sit thou at my right hand, until I make thine enemies thy footstool.*

Matt 22:44 *The LORD said unto my Lord, Sit thou on my right hand, till I make thine enemies thy footstool?*

Mark 12:36 *For David himself said by the Holy Ghost, The LORD said to my Lord, Sit thou on my right hand, till I make thine enemies thy footstool.*

Luke 20:42 *And David himself saith in the book of Psalms, The LORD said unto my Lord, Sit thou on my right hand,* **Luke 20:43** *Till I make thine enemies thy footstool.*

Acts 2:34 *For David is not ascended into the heavens: but he saith himself, The LORD said unto my Lord, Sit thou on my right hand,* **35** *Until I make thy foes thy footstool.*

*Note: This passage (**Acts 2:34-35**) is used to defend the resurrection of Christ.*

The True Nature and Purpose of Angels

Heb 1:14 Are they not all ministering spirits, sent forth to minister for them who shall be heirs of salvation?

Note: (angels) [#32][186x][angels-179; messengers-7] [2465-1 time]

Their natural state is described in v. 7 & v. 14

[Ministers; spirits; messengers; a flame of fire; angels]

Note: The true purpose of angels is to minister to those who shall be heirs of salvation. The angels are appointed to minster to every living believer on the planet. Notice the following passages of scripture:

(Rom 8:16) *The Spirit itself beareth witness with our spirit, that we are the children of God:* **(Rom 8:17)** *And* **if children, then heirs; heirs of God, and joint-heirs with Christ**; *if so be that we suffer with him, that we may be also glorified together.*

(Jas 2:5) *Hearken, my beloved brethren, Hath not God chosen the poor of this world rich in faith, and* **heirs of the kingdom** *which he hath promised to them that love him?*

Note: Because being an heir works through death, here is how it works for the believer. Because Jesus died for us and we put our faith and trust in Jesus to be our Savior, we will receive heaven and the things in heaven when we die so we are joint-heirs with Christ.

4

Hebrews Chapter 2

Heed What We Hear

Heb 2:1 Therefore we ought to give the more earnest heed to the things which we have heard, lest at any time we should let [them] slip.

> Note: "let slip" [3901][1x] We can't afford to forget anything that we have been taught from God's word.

> **Luke 12:48** For unto whomsoever much is given, of him shall be much required:

Heb 2:2 For if the word spoken by angels was stedfast, and every transgression and disobedience received a just **recompence of reward**;

> Note: See Heb. 10:35; 11:26 on "recompense of reward" (or payment)

> **Heb 10:35** Cast not away therefore your confidence, which hath great **recompence of reward.**

Heb 11:26 *Esteeming the reproach of Christ greater riches than the treasures in Egypt: for he had respect unto the <u>recompence of the reward</u>.*

High Price of Neglect

Heb 2:3 <u>**How shall we escape**</u>, if we neglect so great salvation; which at the first began to be spoken by the Lord, and was confirmed unto us by them that heard [him];

Note: C.R. "escape" [There is no escape.]

Rom 2:3 *And thinkest thou this, O man, that judgest them which do such things, and doest the same, that thou shalt escape the judgment of God?*

Note: "neglect" [#272][5x][made light of; regard not; negligent; neglect-2]

[To make light of the things of God is also neglecting them.]

Note: The man that neglects salvation will burn forever in the Lake of Fire.

Purpose of the Gifts of the Holy Ghost
Credentials for the Apostles and Prophets

Heb 2:4 God <u>also bearing [them] witness</u>, both with signs and wonders, and with divers miracles, and <u>gifts of the Holy Ghost</u>, according to his own will?

Note: "signs" [4592][77x][sign 50, miracle 23, wonder 3, token]

Note: "miracles" [1411][120x][power 77, mighty work 11, strength 7, miracle 7, might 4, virtue 3, mighty 2, misc 9]

Note: "gifts" [3311][2x][Heb. 4:12 - dividing asunder]

*Note: The signs, wonders, miracles, and gifts of the Holly Ghost were given specifically to "bear witness" and "confirm the word" **Mark 16:20**.*

Mark 16:17 *And these signs shall follow them that believe; In my name shall they <u>cast out devils</u>; they shall <u>speak with new tongues</u>; 18 They shall <u>take up serpents</u>; and <u>if they drink any deadly thing, it shall not hurt them</u>; <u>they shall lay hands on the sick, and they shall recover.</u>*

Mark 16:20 *And they went forth, and preached every where, the Lord working with them, and **<u>confirming the word with signs following</u>**. Amen.*

The signs and gifts were the credentials of the apostles and prophets and those witnessing and backed up their preaching like the Bible is our backup for us today.

Credentials of Christ

*Note: See **Mat. 11:2-5; Luke 7:20-22** Jesus tells the messengers of John of His credentials. They were never meant to put on a show or to have a so-called healing campaign.*

Matthew 11:2-5 *Now when John had heard in the prison the works of Christ, he sent two of his disciples,* **3** *And said unto him, Art thou he that should come, or do we look for another?* **4** *Jesus answered and said unto them, Go and shew John again those things which ye do hear and see:* **5** <u>**The blind receive their sight, and the lame walk, the lepers are cleansed, and the deaf hear, the dead are raised up, and the poor have the gospel preached to them.**</u>

Luke 7:20 *When the men were come unto him, they said, John Baptist hath sent us unto thee, saying, Art thou he that should come? or look we for another?* **21** *And in that same hour* <u>**he cured many of their infirmities and plagues, and of evil spirits; and unto many that were blind he gave sight**</u>. **22** *Then Jesus answering said unto them, Go your way, and tell John what things ye have seen and heard*<u>**; how that the blind see, the lame walk, the lepers are cleansed, the deaf hear, the dead are raised, to the poor the gospel is preached.**</u>

The list of signs given in **Mark 16:17-18** *are called the signs of the apostles in* **II Cor. 12:12** *"Truly the* <u>**signs of an apostle**</u> *were wrought among you in all patience, in signs, and wonders, and mighty deeds."*

Even during the Old Testament times, the occurrence of miracles was not a common everyday occurrence.

Luke 4:24-27 *And he said, Verily I say unto you, No prophet is accepted in his own country.* **25** *But I tell you of a truth, many widows were in Israel in the days of Elias,* *when the heaven was shut up three years and six months, when great famine was throughout all the land; 26 But unto none of them was Elias sent, save unto Sarepta, a city of Sidon, unto a woman that was a widow. 27 And **many lepers were in Israel in the time of Eliseus the prophet; and none of them was cleansed, saving Naaman the Syrian.***

The Angels and the World to Come

Heb 2:5 For unto the angels hath he not put in subjection the world to come, whereof we speak.

Jesus versus Angels and Man

Heb 2:6 But one in a certain place testified, saying, <u>What is man, that thou art mindful of him? or the son of man, that thou visitest him?</u>

*Note: C.R. v. 6-8 from **Ps 8:4** What is man, that thou art mindful of him? and the son of man, that thou visitest him? 5 For thou hast made him a little lower than the angels, and hast crowned him with glory and honour. 6 Thou madest him to have dominion over the works of thy hands; thou hast put all things under his feet:*

Heb 2:7 <u>Thou madest him a little lower than the angels; thou crownedst him with glory and honour, and didst set him over the works of thy hands:</u>

Heb 2:8 <u>Thou hast put all things in subjection under his feet</u>. For in that he put all in subjection under him, he left nothing [that is] not put under him. But now we see not yet all things put under him.

Heb 2:9 But we see **Jesus, who was made a little lower than the angels for the suffering of death**, crowned with glory and honour; that **he by the grace of God should taste death for every man.**

> *Note: Jesus died on the cross for every man and not just for those who are going to believe the gospel.*

> *1 Timothy 2:3-6 For this is good and acceptable in the sight of God our Saviour; 4 Who will have **all men** to be saved, and to come unto the knowledge of the truth. 5 For there is one God, and one mediator between God and men, the man Christ Jesus; 6 Who gave himself **a ransom for all**, to be testified in due time.*

> *1 Timothy 4:10 For therefore we both labour and suffer reproach, because we trust in **the living God, who is the Saviour of all men, specially of those that believe**.*

> *1 John 2:2 And **he is the propitiation for our sins: and not for ours only, but also for the sins of the whole world.***

> *2 Peter 2:1 But there were false prophets also among the people, even as there shall be false teachers among you, who privily shall bring in damnable heresies, **even denying the Lord that bought them**, and bring upon themselves swift destruction.*

Jesus Is Captain, Prince, And Author of Salvation

Heb 2:10 For it became him, for whom [are] all things, and by whom [are] all things, in bringing many sons unto glory, to make the **captain** of their salvation perfect through sufferings.

*Note: "captain" [747][4x][Prince - **Acts 3:15; 5:31**; Author - **Heb. 12:2** and here as captain]*

*(**Acts 3:15**) And killed the **Prince of life**, whom God hath raised from the dead; whereof we are witnesses.*

*(**Acts 5:31**) Him hath God exalted with his right hand to be a **Prince** and a Saviour, for to give repentance to Israel, and forgiveness of sins.*

*(**Heb 12:2**) Looking unto Jesus **the author** and finisher of our faith; who for the joy that was set before him endured the cross, despising the shame, and is set down at the right hand of the throne of God.*

All of these scripture references refer to Jesus.

The Sanctifier versus the Sanctified
Jesus Calls the Believers "Brethren"

Heb 2:11 For both he that sanctifieth and they who are sanctified [are] all of one: for which cause he is not ashamed to call them brethren,

Note: "sanctifieth" [#37][29x][sanctify-26; Hallowed-2; holy]

Heb 2:12 Saying, I will declare thy name **unto my brethren**, in the midst of the **church** will I sing praise unto thee.

> *Note: C.R.* **Ps 22:22** *I will declare thy name **unto my brethren**: in the midst of the **congregation** will I praise thee.*

Heb 2:13 And again, **I will put my trust in him**. And again, **Behold I and the children which God hath given me.**

> *Note: C.R.* **Ps 7:1** *O LORD my God, **in thee do I put my trust**: save me from all them that persecute me, and deliver me:*

> **Ps 16:1** *Preserve me, O God: for **in thee do I put my trust**.*

> **Ps 56:4** *In God I will praise his word, **in God I have put my trust**; I will not fear what flesh can do unto me.*

> **Ps 56:11** **In God have I put my trust**: *I will not be afraid what man can do unto me.*

> **Ps 73:28** *But it is good for me to draw near to God: **I have put my trust in the Lord GOD**, that I may declare all thy works.*

> **Isa 8:18** **Behold, I and the children whom the LORD hath given me** *are for signs and for wonders in Israel from the LORD of hosts, which dwelleth in mount Zion.*

Jesus Partaker of Flesh and Blood
Heb 2:14 Forasmuch then as the children are partakers of **flesh and blood, he also himself likewise took part of the**

same; that through death he might destroy him that had the power of death, that is, the devil;

Note: One of the reasons that Jesus died was to destroy Satan.

Jesus came in the flesh.

***1John 4:2** Hereby know ye the Spirit of God**: Every spirit that confesseth that Jesus Christ is come in the flesh is of God**: **3** And **every spirit that confesseth not that Jesus Christ is come in the flesh is not of God**: and this is that spirit of antichrist, whereof ye have heard that it should come; and even now already is it in the world.*

***2John 1:7** For **many deceivers are entered into the world, who confess not that Jesus Christ is come in the flesh**. This is a deceiver and an antichrist.*

Luke 24:36** And as they thus spake, **Jesus himself** stood in the midst of them, and saith unto them, Peace be unto you. **Luke 24:37** But they were terrified and affrighted, and supposed that they had seen a spirit. **Luke 24:38** And he said unto them, Why are ye troubled? and why do thoughts arise in your hearts? **Luke 24:39

Behold my hands and my feet, that it is I myself: handle me, and see; for a spirit hath not flesh and bones, as ye see me have.

Note: Jesus did not arise a spirit being, Jesus arose bodily.

Heb 2:15 And deliver them who through fear of death were all their lifetime subject to bondage.

Note: Jesus makes us free from bondage.

John 8:32 *And ye shall know the truth, and **the truth shall make you free***.

John 8:33 *They answered him, We be Abraham's seed, and were never in bondage to any man: how sayest thou, Ye shall be made free?*

John 8:36 ***If the Son therefore shall make you free, ye shall be free indeed***.

Heb 2:16 For verily he took not on [him the nature of] angels; but **he took on [him] the seed of Abraham.**

Note: C.R. ***Phil 2:5*** *Let this mind be in you, which was also in Christ Jesus:* ***6*** *Who, being in the form of God, thought it not robbery to **be equal with God**:* ***7*** *But made himself of no reputation, and **took upon him the form of a servant, and was made in the likeness of men**:* ***8*** *And being found in fashion as a man, he humbled himself, and became obedient unto death, even the death of the cross.* ***9*** *Wherefore God also hath highly exalted him, and given him a name which is above every name:* ***10*** ***That at the name of Jesus** **every knee should bow**, of things in heaven, and things in earth, and things under the earth;* ***11*** *And that **every tongue should confess that Jesus Christ is Lord,** to the glory of God the Father.*

Jesus, The Faithful High Priest

Heb 2:17 Wherefore in all things it **behoved** him to be made like unto [his] brethren, that he might be a merciful and faithful high priest in things [pertaining] to God, to make **reconciliation** for the sins of the people.

Note: "behoved" [3784][36x][owed-7; debt-2; duty-2; ought-15; bound-2; be guilty; misc-7]

Note: "reconciliation" [2433][2x][merciful - Luke 18:13]

Note: One of the reasons for Jesus dying for us was to make "reconciliation for the sins of the people."

Heb 2:18 For in that he himself hath suffered being tempted, he is able to succour them that are tempted.

Note: "succour" [#997][8x][help-6; succour-2]

Note: Jesus is our helper in time of temptation and trials.

(Ps 46:1) *God is our refuge and strength, **a very present help in trouble**.*

5

Hebrew Chapter 3

Jesus Is the Apostle and High Priest

Heb 3:1 Wherefore, holy brethren, **partakers** of the heavenly **calling**, consider the Apostle and High Priest of our profession, Christ Jesus;

Note: "partakers" [#3353][6x][partners; fellows; partaker-4]

Note: "calling" [#2821][11x][vocation - Eph. 4:1; 'calling'-10]

Note: Jesus is the Apostle & the High Priest of our profession.

A Partial List of Cardinal Doctrines
(See this author's book on "Cardinal Doctrines"

1. Jesus is the Christ
2. Jesus is the Son of God
3. Jesus is God the Son
4. Jesus came in Human flesh through the virgin birth

5. Jesus died on the cross and was buried and resurrected to pay for our sins
6. Jesus provided the only blood atonement
7. The Trinity, God the Father, God the Son and God the Holy Spirit
8. Jesus and what He did on the cross is the only way to heaven.
9. The Bible is the word of God.
10. The Gospel is the death, burial, and resurrection of Christ.

Note: One of the privileges of being saved is that we have a vocation from God, a real purpose and calling in life that is God's will for each believer.

Heb 3:2 Who was faithful to him that appointed him, as also Moses [was faithful] in all his house.

Jesus is Better Than Moses

Heb 3:3 For this [man] was counted worthy of more glory than Moses, inasmuch as he who hath builded the house hath more honour than the house.

Note: Jesus is better than Moses as the creator is better than the creation and as the builder is better than the building.

John 5:46 *For had ye believed Moses, ye would have believed me: for he wrote of me.*

Heb 3:4 For every house is builded by some [man]; but he that built all things [is] God.

Note: "Every house is built by some man" tells us there is no such thing as evolution. The building declares the builder. The painting declares the painter and the creation declares the creator.

The Servant versus the Son

Heb 3:5 And Moses verily [was] faithful in all his house, as a servant, for a testimony of those things which were to be spoken after;

Note: Comparing Moses as servant and Jesus as the Son of God:

Genuine Faith Is Not Temporary

Heb 3:6 But Christ as a son over his own house; whose house are we, <u>if we **hold fast** the **confidence** and the rejoicing of the **hope firm** unto the **end.**</u>

*Note: (#2722) "hold fast" (19x)(hold fast-3; hold-3; keep-2; **possess**-2; take; have; make; seize; stayed; misc-4)*

(#3954) "confindence" (31x)("confidence-6; boldness-8; plainly-4;openly-4; confidence-6; freely; misc-2)

(#1680) "hope" (54x)(hope-53; "faith"-1)

(#949) "firm"(9x)(firm; sure; stedfast-4; firm; of force; more sure)

> (#5056) "end" (42x)(end-35; uttermost; finally; custom-3;ending; misc-1)

Note: If a person is genuinely saved, as a result, they will "hold the beginning of their confidence steadfast unto the end." They will not be looking for anything else to save them but Jesus. Genuine faith brings genuine salvation. A true test of genuine salvation is what we are depending on to get us to heaven through time. If it is a temporary belief, it is not a genuine faith and we will have a tendency to add to our temporary belief, works and deeds that we do to help get us into heaven. It is a mere consideration. Study the following passages. Remember salvation is instant the moment you trust Christ as Savior. However, when you put your faith in Christ to be your Savior, not only are you given eternal life immediately, you will not look for anything else to save you.

> **Heb. 10:38** *Now the just shall live by faith: but if [any man] draw back, my soul shall have no pleasure in him.* **39** *But we are not of them who draw back unto perdition; but of them that believe to the saving of the soul.*

> **1 John 2:19** *They went out from us, but they were not of us; for if they had been of us, they would [no doubt] have continued with us: but [they went out], that they might be made manifest that they were not all of us.*

Temporary Faith or Mere Consideration versus Genuine Faith

Temporary Faith

Luke 8:13 *They on the rock are they, which, when they hear, receive the word with joy; and these have no root,* ***which for a while believe****, and in time of temptation fall away.*

Luke 16:30 *And he said, Nay, father Abraham: but if one went unto them from the dead, they will* ***repent****. **31** And he said unto him, If they hear not Moses and the prophets, neither will they* ***be persuaded****, though one rose from the dead.*

Note: Not only must the mind be changed, it has to be made up or fixed or persuaded.

Temporary Faith

Acts 28:6 *Howbeit they looked when he should have swollen, or fallen down dead suddenly: but after they had looked a great while, and saw no harm come to him, they* ***changed their minds****, and said that he was a god.*

Note: The change of mind here is not "metanoeo" change of mind. It is an ***impulsive*** *change of mind.*

Genuine Faith

John 3:15-16 *That whosoever **believeth** in him should not perish, but have eternal life. **16** For God so loved the world, that he gave his only begotten Son, that whosoever **believeth** in him should not perish, but have everlasting life.*

Note: The verbs "believeth" #4100 (248x)(believe 239, commit unto 4, commit to (one's) trust; be committed unto; be put in trust with; be commit to one's trust; believer)

*Verb tense: #5723 **present tense** which is **continuous action***

High Price of a Hard Heart

Heb 3:7 Wherefore (as the Holy Ghost saith, To day if ye will hear his voice,

Heb 3:8 Harden not your hearts, as in the provocation, in the day of temptation in the wilderness:

Heb 3:9 When your fathers tempted me, proved me, and saw my works forty years.

Heb 3:10 Wherefore I was grieved with that generation, and said, They do alway err in [their] heart; and they have not known my ways.

The Rest for the People of God

Heb 3:11 So I sware in my wrath, They shall not enter into my **rest**.)

Note: C.R. for v. 7-11

Ps 95:7 For he is our God; and we are the people of his pasture, and the sheep of his hand. To day if ye will hear his voice, 8 Harden not your heart, as in the provocation, and as in the day of temptation in the wilderness: 9 When your fathers tempted me, proved me, and saw my work. 10 Forty years long was I grieved with this generation, and said, It is a people that do err in their heart, and they have not known my ways: 11 Unto whom I sware in my wrath that they should not enter into my rest.

The Danger of Unbelief

Heb 3:12 Take heed, brethren, lest there be in any of you an **evil heart of unbelief**, in **departing #868** from the living God.

Note: John 3:18 He that believeth on him is not condemned: but __he that believeth not is condemned already__, because he hath not believed in the name of the only begotten Son of God.

John 3:36 He that believeth on the Son hath everlasting life: __and he that believeth not the Son shall not see life; but the wrath of God abideth on him__.

John 16:8 *And when he is come, he will reprove the world of __sin__, and of righteousness, and of judgment: __9__ Of __sin, because they believe not on me__; __10__ Of righteousness, because I go to my Father, and ye see me no more; __11__ Of judgment, because the prince of this world is judged.*

Note: "departing" [#868][15x][fall away-__Luke 8:13__; drew away; refrain; withdraw thyself; away; depart-10]

Note: The one sin that the Holy Spirit will convict a lost person of is unbelief.

Luke 8:13 *They on the rock are they, which, when they hear, receive the word with joy; and these have no root, which __for a while believe__, and in time of temptation __fall away__.*

Note: (__2Cor 13:5__) __Examine yourselves, whether ye be in the faith__; prove your own selves. Know ye not your own selves, how that Jesus Christ is in you, except ye be reprobates?

(Make sure you are saved. Study Chapter 1 of this book.)

Heb 3:13 But exhort one another daily, while it is called To day; lest any of you be __hardened through the deceitfulness of sin.__

Note: Of the many dangerous characteristics and effects of sin, the deceiving power of sin is one of the most dangerous and it hardens the individual and calluses them toward the things of God.

Note: **Matt 24:12** *And because iniquity shall abound, the love of many shall wax cold.*

Genuine Faith Is Not Temporary, it is Permanently set on Jesus
(See notes at verse 6)

Heb 3:14 For we are made **partakers #3353** of Christ, <u>if we hold the beginning of our **confidence #5287** stedfast unto the end;</u>

Note: (#3353) "partakers" (6x)(fellows; partners; partakers-4)

(#5287) "confidence" (5x)(3x confidence; person Heb. 1:3; Heb. 11:1 substance)

Heb 3:15 While it is said, To day if ye will hear his voice, harden not your hearts, as in the provocation.

Heb 3:16 For some, when they had heard, did provoke: howbeit not all that came out of Egypt by Moses.

Heb 3:17 But with whom was he grieved forty years? [was it] not with them that had sinned, whose carcasses fell in the wilderness?

Unbelief Stops Us from Entering into the Rest

Heb 3:18 And to whom sware he that they should not enter into his **rest**, but to them that **believed not**?

Note: One of the reasons Moses had so much trouble with the children of Israel in the wilderness is because many of them were lost or unbelievers.

Note: What the Rest or the Promised Land represents for Christians today.

3:11	*[It is God's rest.]*
3:18, 19; 4:6	*[Unbelief stops people from entering into this rest.]*
4:1	*[Some should seem to come short of it.]*
4:3	*[Those who have believed do enter into this rest.]*
4:9	*[The rest is future for the people of God.]*
4:10	*[Once entered in he has ceased from his own works.]*
4:11	*[Let us labor (study; be diligent) to enter into that rest.]*
4:11	*[Lest any man fall after the same example of unbelief.]*

Note: Conclusion: The rest is heaven for the children of God compared in type with the Old Testament 'promised land' to the Israelite.

Heb 3:19 So we see that they could not enter in because of **unbelief**.

Note: **John 3:18** *He that believeth on him is not condemned:* **<u>but he that believeth not is condemned already, because he hath not believed in the name of the only begotten Son of God.</u>**

John 3:36 *He that believeth on the Son hath everlasting life: and* **<u>he that believeth not the Son shall not see life; but the wrath of God abideth on him.</u>**

6

Hebrews Chapter 4

Proper Fear and Genuine Faith

Heb 4:1 Let us therefore fear, lest, a promise being left [us] of entering into his <u>rest</u>, any of you should seem to come short of it.

Salvation has Always Been the Same
(By Faith in Christ)

Heb 4:2 For <u>unto us was the gospel preached, as well as unto them</u>: but the word preached did not profit them, <u>not being mixed with faith </u>in them that heard [it].

Note: "not being mixed with faith" Allow me to illustrate this point. The gospel is like light. One of the facts about light is that if the light does not hit anything you cannot see it. If the gospel is not believed it will do you no good.

Note: The gospel was preached to people in the Old Testament like it is preached now. Salvation has always been the same. Study the following passages.

Note: **Romans 4:1-11** *What shall we say then that* **<u>Abraham</u>** *our father, as pertaining to the flesh, hath found?* **2** **<u>For if Abraham were justified by works, he hath whereof to glory; but not before God</u>.** **3** *For what saith the scripture?* **<u>Abraham believed God, and it was counted unto him for righteousness</u>.** **4** *Now to him that worketh is the reward not reckoned of grace, but of debt.* **5** *But to him that worketh not, but believeth on him that justifieth the ungodly, his faith is counted for righteousness.* **6** *Even as* **<u>David</u>** *also describeth the blessedness of the man, unto whom* **<u>God imputeth righteousness without works</u>,** **7** *Saying, Blessed are they whose iniquities are forgiven, and whose sins are covered.* **8** *Blessed is the man to whom the Lord will not impute sin.* **9** *Cometh this blessedness then upon the circumcision only, or upon the uncircumcision also? for we say that faith was reckoned to Abraham for righteousness.* **10** *How was it then reckoned? when he was in circumcision, or in uncircumcision? Not in circumcision, but in uncircumcision.* **11** *And he received the sign of circumcision, a seal of the righteousness of the faith which he had yet being uncircumcised: that he might be the father of all them that believe, though they be not circumcised; that righteousness might be imputed unto them also:*

Galatians 3:6-8 *Even as* **<u>Abraham believed God, and it was accounted to him for righteousness</u>.** **7** *Know* *ye therefore that they which are of faith, the same are the children of Abraham. **8** And the scripture, foreseeing that God would justify the heathen through faith, **<u>preached before the gospel unto Abraham</u>**, saying, In thee shall all nations be blessed.*

Animal Sacrifices Had no Part in Salvation

Hebrews 9:9 *Which was a figure for the time then present, in which were offered both gifts and sacrifices, that could not make him that did the service perfect, as pertaining to the conscience;*

Hebrews 10:4 *For it is not possible that the blood of bulls and of goats should take away sins.*

John 8:56 *Your father **<u>Abraham rejoiced to see my day: and he saw it, and was glad.</u>***

Genesis 22:8 *And Abraham said, My son, God will provide himself **<u>a lamb</u>** for a burnt offering: so they went both of them together.*

Note: That Lamb is Jesus.

John 1:29 *The next day John seeth Jesus coming unto him, and saith, **<u>Behold the Lamb of God, which taketh away the sin of the world.</u>***

John 1:36 *And looking upon Jesus as he walked, he saith, **<u>Behold the Lamb of God</u>**!*

Acts 8:32 *The place of the scripture which he read was this,* **He was led as a sheep to the slaughter; and like a lamb dumb before his shearer, so opened he not his mouth:**

I Pet 1:18 *Forasmuch as ye know that* ***ye were*** *not* **redeemed** *with corruptible things, as silver and gold, from your vain conversation received by tradition from your fathers;* ***1Pet 1:19*** *But* **with the precious blood of Christ, as of a lamb without blemish and without spot:**

Belief Takes us into the Rest

Heb 4:3 For we which have believed do enter into rest, as he said, As I have sworn in my wrath, if they shall enter into my **rest**: although the works were finished from the foundation of the world.

Note: See ***Heb. 3:18*** *for notes on "the rest"*

Note: "foundation" #2602 [11 times][10-foundation; 1-conceive]

Heb 4:4 For he spake in a certain place of the seventh [day] on this wise, And God did **rest** the seventh day from all his works.

Note: C.R. ***Gen 2:2*** *And on the seventh day God ended his work which he had made; and he rested on the seventh day from all his work which he had made.*

Heb 4:5 And in this [place] again, If they shall enter into my **rest**.

Unbelief Stops Us from Entering into Rest

Heb 4:6 Seeing therefore it remaineth that some must enter therein, and they to whom it was first preached entered not in **because of unbelief**:

Note: See notes at **Heb. 3:18**

Heb 4:7 Again, he limiteth a certain day, saying in David, To day, after so long a time; as it is said, Today if ye will hear his voice, harden not your hearts.

Note: C.R. **Ps 95:7** *For he is our God; and we are the people of his pasture, and the sheep of his hand.* <u>To day if ye will hear his voice,</u> **8** <u>Harden not your heart</u>, *as in the provocation, and as in the day of temptation in the wilderness:*

Heb 4:8 For if **Jesus** had given them **rest**, then would he not afterward have spoken of another day.

Note: "Jesus" here at this point is referring to Joshua.

The Rest Is Future for The People of God

Heb 4:9 There remaineth therefore a **rest** to the people of God.

The Rest Is Where our Works Cease

Heb 4:10 For he that is entered into his <u>rest</u>, he also hath ceased from his own works, as God [did] from his.

> *Note: "ceased from his own works" This can be seen twofold. The unbeliever that is trying to good deed his way to heaven but then comes to the reality that he cannot good deed his way to heaven because his good deeds cannot pay for his sin. When he realizes that Jesus died for his sin and has paid for all his sins, then he trusts Christ to be his savior and ceasing to try to work his way into heaven. He has ceased from his own works, trying to do them to get to heaven.*

> *In the believer, when he dies, he goes to heaven because of trusting Christ as Savior, he has ceased from his own works and service he does for God in this life. However, the influence of his works continues. He serves God in this life because he loves God and not because he thinks it will help him get to heaven. Jesus said the following.*

> **John 14:15** *If ye love me, keep my commandments.*

Be Diligent to Enter into that Rest

Heb 4:11 Let us labour therefore to enter into that <u>rest</u>, lest any man fall after the same example of <u>**unbelief**</u>.

> *Note: "labour" [4704][11 times][study-II Tim. 2:15; some form of 'diligent'-5; endeavour-3; be forward-1; labour-1]*

The Word of God

Heb 4:12 For the word of God [is] quick, and powerful, and sharper than any twoedged sword, piercing even to the dividing asunder of soul and spirit, and of the joints and marrow, and [is] a discerner of the thoughts and intents of the heart.

Note: The power of the Word of God must never be underestimated.

Isaiah 55:11 So shall my word be that goeth forth out of my mouth: it shall not return unto me void, but it shall accomplish that which I please, and it shall prosper in the thing whereto I sent it.

Jeremiah 23:29 Is not my word like as a fire? saith the LORD; and like a hammer that breaketh the rock in pieces?

Note: "quick" simply means "alive or living"

Note: The human being is made of "body, soul, and spirit"

See this author's book on "What the Bible says about Death" and Chapter 5 for a thorough study and the body, soul, and spirit.

*1Thess 5:23 And the very God of peace sanctify you wholly; and I pray God your whole **spirit** and **soul** and **body** be preserved blameless unto the coming of our Lord Jesus Christ.*

1) *Body: the sense conscience, containing our five physical senses*
2) *Soul: the self-conscience and the seat of our emotions*
3) *Spirit: The God consciousness, the part of us that communes with God*

Note: Another thing that is pointed out in Heb. 4:12 is the fact that the Bible can read our minds. In other words, the Bible can tell us what we are thinking. The Bible even tells us our motive for doing the things that we do. Notice the following examples:

John 3:19 *And this is the condemnation, that light is come into the world, and* **men loved darkness rather than light, because their deeds were evil.**

1John 4:19 **We love him, because he first loved us**.

The Eyes of God Sees All

Heb 4:13 Neither is there any creature that is not manifest in his sight: but all things [are] naked and opened unto the eyes of him with whom we have to do.

Note: God sees all. He sees every heart and mind of every individual.

Prov 15:3 *The eyes of the LORD are in every place, beholding the evil and the good.*

__Prov 5:21__ For the ways of man are before the eyes of the LORD, and he pondereth all his goings.

__Ps 33:14__ From the place of his habitation he looketh upon all the inhabitants of the earth.

The Son of God as the Great High Priest

Heb 4:14 Seeing then that we have a great high priest, that is passed into the heavens, Jesus the Son of God, let us hold fast [our] profession.

Note: He is not referring to holding on to your salvation. God does that.

He is saying not to doubt your salvation but to claim and cling to the promises of God.

__1John 2:25__ And __this is the promise that he hath promised us, even eternal life__.

The Compassion of God and Great High Priest

Heb 4:15 For we have not an high priest which cannot be **touched** with the feeling of our **infirmities**; but was in all points tempted like as [we are, yet] without sin.

Note: Jesus not only sees and knows all your needs, v.14; v.15 __He feels all your needs__.

Note: "touched" [#4834][2x][Heb. 10:34-had compassion of]

Note: "infirmities" [#769][24x][sickness; diseases; weakness-5; infirmity-17]

Note: Since Jesus was tempted, it is not a sin to be tempted, but it is a sin to yield to temptation. Again, since Jesus is touched with the feeling of our infirmities, Jesus does not just know your pain, He also feels your pain.

The Throne of God is the Throne of Grace

Heb 4:16 Let us therefore come boldly unto the throne of grace, that we may obtain mercy, and find **grace to help in time of need**.

Note: Grace is not only what we need, grace will be there in the time of need. For example, if the need is not their yet, neither is the grace for that need. A believer cannot expect dying grace until the believer in dying.

Note: Please understand "boldly" does not mean "arrogantly."

*"boldly" #3954 (31x)(boldness-8; **confidence**-6; openly-4; plainly-4; misc-9)*

7

Hebrews Chapter 5

The High Priest

Heb 5:1 For every high priest taken from among men is **ordained** for men in things [pertaining] to God, that he may offer both gifts and sacrifices for sins:

Note: "ordained" [#2525][22x][hath made ruler-6; appoint-1; conducted-1; be-2; set-1; ordain-3; make-8]

Heb 5:2 Who can have compassion on the ignorant, and on them that **are out of the way**; for that he himself also is compassed with **infirmity**.

Note: "are out of the way" [#4105][39x][gone astray-5; do err-6; deceive-24; seduce-2; wandered; be out of the way]

Note: "infirmities" [#769][24x][sickness; diseases; weakness-5; infirmity-17]

Heb 5:3 And by reason hereof he ought, as <u>for the people, so also for himself</u>, to offer for sins.

The Priest Must Be Called of God

Heb 5:4 And no man taketh this honour unto himself, but he that is called of God, as [was] Aaron.

> *Note: "honour" [#5092][45x][honor-35; price-8; sum; precious]*

> *Note: Although a child of God must be willing to do anything God leads him to do, a man cannot volunteer to preach or take up preaching because it seems like it is a good thing to do. He must be called of God to preach, and not be called by parents or other preachers and not to take this honor unto himself.*

Jesus, The High Priest

Heb 5:5 So also Christ glorified not himself to be made an high priest; but he that said unto him, Thou art my Son, to day have I begotten thee.

> *Note: C.R.* **Ps 2:7** *I will declare the decree: the LORD hath said unto me, Thou art my Son; this day have I begotten thee.*

> *Note: Jesus did not make himself a high priest, but was called by God the Father to be the high priest.*

Jesus with A Priesthood after the Order of Melchisedec

Heb 5:6 As he saith also in another [place], Thou [art] a priest for ever after the order of **Melchisedec**.

Note: The order is that Melchisedec and Christ were both kings and priests.

Heb 5:7 <u>Who</u> in the <u>**days of his flesh**</u>, when he had offered up prayers and supplications with strong crying and tears unto him that was able to save him from death, and was heard in that he feared;

The Verses that are Dealing with Melchizedec

*Ps 110:4 The LORD hath sworn, and will not repent, Thou art a priest for ever after the order of **Melchizedek**.*

*Gen 14:17 And the king of Sodom went out to meet him after his return from the slaughter of Chedorlaomer, and of the kings that were with him, at the valley of Shaveh, which is the king's dale. Gen 14:18 And **Melchizedek king of Salem** brought forth bread and wine: and **he was the priest of the most high God**.*

Note: To make Melchizedek literally Jesus is to put Jesus on earth at this time before the virgin birth and before Jesus took on human flesh to be king of Salem and also you have Jesus bringing forth bread and wine to the other kings instead of Melchizedek doing this. (Heb 7:1) The Bible does not say that Jesus was Melchizedek. It does tells us many times that Jesus was high priest after the order of Melchisedec. According to **(Heb 5:7)**, it was Melchisedec who was in the days of his flesh and not Jesus.

Heb 5:6 *As he saith also in another place, Thou art a priest for ever after the order of* **<u>Melchisedec</u>**.

Heb 5:10 *Called of God an high priest after the order of* **<u>Melchisedec</u>**.

Heb 6:20 *Whither the forerunner is for us entered, even Jesus, made an high priest for ever after the order of* **<u>Melchisedec</u>**.

Heb 7:1 *For this* **<u>Melchisedec, king of Salem</u>***, priest of the most high God,* <u>who met Abraham returning from the slaughter of the kings</u>*, and blessed him;*

Heb 7:10 *For he was yet in the loins of his father, when Melchisedec met him.* **11** *If therefore perfection were by the Levitical priesthood, (for under it the people received the law,) what further need was there that another priest should rise after the order of Melchisedec, and not be called after the order of Aaron?*

Heb 7:15 *And it is yet far more evident: for that after the similitude of Melchisedec there ariseth another priest,*

Heb 7:21 *(For those priests were made without an oath; but this with an oath by him that said unto him, The Lord sware and will not repent, Thou art a priest for ever after the order of Melchisedec:)*

Note: Jesus and Melchisedec were both kings and priests however Jesus and Melchisedec are not one and the same. Like Jesus is greater than Moses, Jesus is greater than Melchisedec.

Lessons Through Suffering Well Learned

Heb 5:8 Though he were a Son, yet <u>learned he obedience</u> by the things which he suffered;

Note: God has an amazing way of teaching us obedience by allowing us to suffer. Some obedience and submission can only be learned this way.

Jesus, The Author of Eternal Salvation

Heb 5:9 And being made perfect, he became **the author of eternal salvation unto all them that obey him;**

Note: Jesus is the author of eternal salvation.

Note: "obey" [5219][21x][to hearken-1; obey-18; be obedient-2]

This passage is not referring to obedience to all the commands of God otherwise no one can be saved because all have sinned. It is referring to obedience to the Gospel of Christ by hearkening to it and believing it. Notice the following passages below about obeying the gospel.

> **Acts 6:7** *And the word of God increased; and the number of the disciples multiplied in Jerusalem greatly; and a great company of the priests were __obedient to the faith.__*

> **Rom 6:17** *But God be thanked, that ye were the servants of sin, but ye have __obeyed from the heart that form of doctrine which was delivered you__.*

> **Rom 10:16** *But they have not all __obeyed the gospel__. For Esaias saith, Lord, who hath believed our report?*

> **2 Thess 1:8** *In flaming fire taking vengeance on them that know not God, and that __obey not the gospel of our Lord Jesus Christ__:*

Jesus, A Priest like Melchisedec
King and Priest Together

Heb 5:10 Called of God an high priest after the order of Melchisedec.

> *Note: Jesus is the high priest after the order of Melchisedec.*

The Need to Mature

Heb 5:11 Of whom we have many things to say, and hard to be uttered, seeing ye are dull of hearing.

> *Note: "dull" [#3576][2x][Heb. 6:12 - slothful]*

Note: Sometimes things are hard to be preached and taught not because of the material we are using but because of students who are dull of hearing or lazy listeners.

The Immature Christian Unable to Teach the Word

Heb 5:12 For when for the time ye ought to be teachers, ye have need that one teach you again which [be] the **first** principles of the oracles of God; and are become such as have need of milk, and not of **strong** meat.

Note: He is not saying that the unbeliever ought to teach. He is talking to the believer, but these believers are too immature.

Note: "first" [#746][58x][beginning-40; magistrates; power; corners-2; Principality-8; first-2; misc-4]

Note: "principles" [#4747][7x][elements-4; rudiments-2; principle]

Note: "strong" [#4731][4x][sure; steadfast; strong-2]

The Immature Christian is Unskillful in the Word

Heb 5:13 For every one that useth milk [is] unskilful in the word of righteousness: for he is a **babe**.

Note: "babe" does not mean [a lost person or unbeliever], it means

(#3516)(14x)(babe-6; child-5; children-2; and childish]

A young Christian or new convert or a childish believer.

Example ref. **1Cor 3:1** *And I, brethren, could not speak unto you as unto spiritual, but as unto* ***carnal, even as unto babes in Christ****.*

Note: Skill is only developed in the Word of God as we study the Word.

The Matured in Christ

Heb 5:14 But strong meat belongeth to them that are of **full age**, [even] those who by reason of use have their senses exercised to discern both good and evil.

Note: "full age" [#5046][19x][full age; men; perfect-17]

Note: The more we learn, it enables us to learn more and teach others.

2Tim 2:2 *And the things that thou hast heard of me among many witnesses, the same commit thou to faithful men, who shall be able to teach others also.*

Learning and growing are directly connected. Notice the following passage.

(2Pet 3:18) *But* ***grow in grace, and in the knowledge of our Lord and Saviour Jesus Christ.*** *To him be glory both now and for ever. Amen.*

8

Hebrews Chapter 6

**Building on the Foundation of Basic Doctrine
(A Firm Warning to Those Who Have Matured)**

Heb 6:1 Therefore leaving the **principles of the doctrine of Christ**, let us go on unto perfection; not laying again the foundation of **repentance from dead works, and of faith toward God**,

> *Note: "principles" [#746][58][beginning 40, principality 8, corner 2, first 2, misc 6]*

> *Note: The principles mentioned here were previously mentioned in **Heb 5:12** as the "first principles of the oracles of God" which here are called "principles of the doctrine of Christ" and not Judaism.*

> *The principles as in the foundation or*
> *basic doctrines are as follows:*

1) *Repentance from dead works:*
   Luke 13:3 *I tell you, Nay: but, except ye repent, ye shall all likewise perish.*

   Luke 13:5 *I tell you, Nay: but, except ye repent, ye shall all likewise perish.*

   2Pet 3:9 *The Lord is not slack concerning his promise, as some men count slackness; but is longsuffering to us-ward, not willing that any should perish, but that all should come to repentance.*

   The "dead works" that a person is to repent from is the works and deeds that a person thinks will save them or help get or keep them saved. The person is to change his mind from thinking he must work to get to heaven or work to pay for his own sins to realizing his only hope for heaven is Jesus and the work Jesus did on the cross to pay for his sins. The only sin that the person is to repent from in order to be saved is the sin of "unbelief".

John 3:18 *He that believeth on him is not condemned: but **he that believeth not is condemned already, because he hath not believed in the name of the only begotten Son of God.***

John 3:36 *He that believeth on the Son hath everlasting life: and* **he that believeth not the Son shall not see life; but the wrath of God abideth on him.**

To have the lost sinner to attempt to repent of any other sins besides unbelief would produce reformation instead of regeneration. Please see this author's book on "How to Study the Bible for Yourself" and "Repentance."

   2)   *Faith toward God:*

      John 3:15 *That whosoever believeth in him should not perish, but have eternal life.*

      John 3:16 *For God so loved the world, that he gave his only begotten Son, that whosoever believeth in him should not perish, but have everlasting life.*

      John 3:18 *He that believeth on him is not condemned: but he that believeth not is condemned already, because he hath not believed in the name of the only begotten Son of God.*

      John 3:36 *He that believeth on the Son hath everlasting life: and he that believeth not the Son shall not see life; but the wrath of God abideth on him.*

      John 5:24 *Verily, verily, I say unto you, He that heareth my word, and believeth on him that sent me, hath everlasting life, and shall not come into condemnation; but is passed from death unto life.*

> **John 6:40** *And this is the will of him that sent me, that every one which seeth the Son, and believeth on him, may have everlasting life: and I will raise him up at the last day.*

> **John 6:47** *Verily, verily, I say unto you, He that believeth on me hath everlasting life.*

> **1John 5:13** *These things have I written unto you that believe on the name of the Son of God; that ye may know that ye have eternal life, and that ye may believe on the name of the Son of God.*

Heb 6:2 Of the doctrine of baptisms, and of laying on of hands, and of resurrection of the dead, and of eternal judgment.

> 3) *The doctrine of baptisms [#909][4x][3 times "washing or washings" and once, "baptisms"] Notice below the other three passages that use the word with the Strong's Number #909.*

> **(Mark 7:4)** *And when they come from the market, except they wash, they eat not. And many other things there be, which they have received to hold, as the **washing** of cups, and pots, brasen vessels, and of tables.*

> **(Mark 7:8)** *For laying aside the commandment of God, ye hold the tradition of men, as the **washing** of pots and cups: and many other such like things ye do.*

(Heb 9:10) *Which stood only in meats and drinks, and* **_divers washings_**, *and carnal ordinances, imposed on them until the time of reformation.*

So, the "baptisms" mentioned in **Heb. 6:2** *is not the same as the baptism that pictures the death, burial and resurrection of Christ. The "baptisms" in* **Heb. 6:2** *is referring to ceremonial washings.*

4) *Laying on of hands:*
   2Tim 1:6 *Wherefore I put thee in remembrance that thou stir up the gift of God, which is in thee* **_by the putting on of my hands_**.

   1Tim 4:14 *Neglect not the gift that is in thee, which was given thee by prophecy,* **_with the laying on of the hands_** *of the presbytery.*

   Acts 6:6 *Whom they set before the apostles: and when they had prayed,* **_they laid their hands on them_**.

   Acts 8:17 *Then* **_laid they their hands on them_**, *and they received the Holy Ghost.*

   Acts 9:17 *And Ananias went his way, and entered into the house; and* **_putting his hands on him_** *said, Brother Saul, the Lord, even Jesus, that appeared unto thee in the way as thou camest, hath sent me, that thou mightest receive thy sight, and be filled with the Holy Ghost.*

*Acts 13:3 And when they had fasted and prayed, and **laid their hands on them**, they sent them away.*

*Acts 19:6 And when Paul had **laid his hands upon them**, the Holy Ghost came on them; and they spake with tongues, and prophesied.*

*Acts 28:8 And it came to pass, that the father of Publius lay sick of a fever and of a bloody flux: to whom Paul entered in, and prayed, and **laid his hands on him, and healed him**.*

Note: So, the "laying on of hands" is referring to ceremonial procedures of ordaining, healing, and praying for individuals to be filled with the Holy Spirit.

5) *Resurrection of the dead*
   *Rom 10:9 That if thou shalt confess with thy mouth the Lord Jesus, and shalt **believe in thine heart that God hath raised him from the dead, thou shalt be saved**.*

   I Cor 15:1 *Moreover, brethren, I declare unto you the gospel which I preached unto you, which also ye have received, and wherein ye stand; **2** By which also ye are saved, if ye keep in memory what I preached unto you, unless ye have believed in vain. **3** For I delivered unto you first of all that which I also received, how that **Christ died for our sins according to the scriptures; 4** And*

that he was buried, and that he rose again the third day according to the scriptures:

1Cor 15:12 *Now* ***if Christ be preached that he rose from the dead, how say some among you that there is no resurrection of the dead****?*

6) *Eternal judgment:*

Rev 14:11 *And* **the smoke of their torment ascendeth up for ever and ever***: and they have no rest day nor night, who worship the beast and his image, and whosoever receiveth the mark of his name.*

Rev 20:10 *And the devil that deceived them was cast into the lake of fire and brimstone, where the beast and the false prophet are, and shall be* ***tormented day and night for ever and ever****.*

Jude 1:7 *Even as Sodom and Gomorrha, and the cities about them in like manner, giving themselves over to fornication, and going after strange flesh, are set forth for an example, suffering the* ***vengeance of eternal fire****.*

2Thess 1:9 *Who shall be punished with* **everlasting destruction** *from the presence of the Lord, and from the glory of his power;*

Heb 6:1 *Therefore leaving the principles of the doctrine of Christ,* ***let us go on unto perfection****; not laying* *again the foundation of repentance from dead works, and of faith toward God,*

*Note: "perfection" [5047 - 2 times - **Col. 3:14** "perfectness"]*

Note: The Bible says, "let us" which means the author is including himself in going on to perfection.

*Note: The Greek word for this word "perfection" only appears 2 times in the New Testament, here and in **Col. 3:14**. "perfectness" is referring in **Col. 3:12** to "the elect of God" and their maturing character.*

*The root Greek word for #5047 is #5046 appearing 19 times in the New Testament. One of those times is in **Heb. 5:14** being translated "full age" which is inside the paragraph of the context we are now studying. The other place in the book of Hebrews for this Greek word is in **Heb. 9:11** "a greater and more perfect tabernacle".*

Note: "leaving the principles of the doctrine of Christ" does not mean to abandon them, it means to build on top of these principles just like framing a building on top of a foundation. The definition of "leaving" has the idea of leaving so that what is left may remain or leave remaining.

Heb 6:3 And this will <u>we</u> do, if God permit.

Note: "will we do" The author includes himself again in this passage.

To Whom Much Is Given, Much Is Required

Heb 6:4 For [it is] impossible for those who were once enlightened, and have tasted of the heavenly gift, and were made partakers of the Holy Ghost,

Note: "enlightened" [5461][11x][give light-2; bring to light-2; lighten-2; enlighten-2; light; illuminate; make to see]

*Note: "have tasted" [1089][15x][taste-12; eat-3] (**Heb. 2:9**-Jesus tasted death for every man); (**1Pet 2:3**) If so be ye have tasted that the Lord is gracious.*

Note: "were made partakers of the Holy Ghost" means there was a genuine conversion.

Note it says, "were made partakers of the Holy Ghost". It does not say 'were made partakers of the work of the Holy Ghost'. To be made a partaker of the Holy Ghost is to be saved. A lost person cannot be a partaker of the Holy Ghost. See the following passages.

> **Eph 1:13** *In whom ye also trusted, after that ye heard the word of truth, the gospel of your salvation: in whom also after that ye believed, ye were sealed with that holy Spirit of promise,*

> **Rom 8:9** *But ye are not in the flesh, but in the Spirit, if so be that the Spirit of God dwell in you. **<u>Now if any man have not the Spirit of Christ, he is none of his.</u>***

Note: "partakers" [#3353][6x][partaker-4; fellow; 1 time **Lu. 5:7** *"partners"]*

Heb 6:5 And have tasted the good word of God, and the powers of the world to come,

> *Note: To taste the Word of God and taste the powers of the world to come is not referring to unbelievers. Neither is it referring to the new convert or the carnal Christian. These are not only believers but also believers with maturity and are given leadership positions and positions of great responsibility.*

> > **Heb 5:14** *But strong meat belongeth to **them that are of full age**, even those who by reason of use have their senses exercised to discern both good and evil.*

> > **Heb 6:1** *Therefore leaving the principles of the doctrine of Christ, **let us go on unto perfection**; not laying again the foundation of repentance from dead works, and of faith toward God,*

Heb 6:6 If they shall fall away, to <u>renew them again</u> unto repentance; seeing they crucify to themselves the Son of God afresh, and put [him] to an open shame.

> *Note: "fall away" [#3895 -1 time- def. deviate from right path][not the same as in II Thess. 2:3 (#646-"apostasia") (fall away; forsake-Acts 21:21)*

> *Note: "renew" [#340 -1 time- def. renovate] [this does not mean forgive]*

Note: "open shame"[#3856][2x][Mat. 1:19 "make a public example"]

Note: The falling away here is not apostasy. It is a matured responsible believer getting off on the wrong path and into open sin and losing his position of service. It will be impossible for him to get that position of service back.

Heb 6:7 For the earth which drinketh in the rain that cometh oft upon it, and bringeth forth herbs meet for them by whom it is dressed, receiveth blessing from God

Note: This is not two different kinds of ground, it is two different kinds of fruit coming from the same ground. (good versus bad)(herbs versus thorns &briers)

Heb 6:8 But that which beareth thorns and briers [is] rejected, and [is] nigh unto cursing; whose end [is] to be burned.

Note: That which is to be burned is the thorns and briers off the land and not burning the land itself to destroy the land.

Note: v. 8 "burned" is referring to the fire at the Judgment Seat of Christ.

> *1Cor 3:12 Now if any man build upon this foundation gold, silver, precious stones, wood, hay, stubble; 13 Every man's work shall be made manifest: for the day shall declare it, because it shall be revealed by fire; and **the fire shall try every man's work of what sort it is.** 14 If any man's work abide which he hath built*

*thereupon, he shall receive a reward. **15** If any man's work shall be burned, he shall suffer loss: but he himself shall be saved; yet so as by fire.*

At the Judgment Seat Of Christ [herbs as 'gold, silver, or precious stone' and thorns & briers as 'wood, hay, and stubble] **<u>When you burn a field off, you are not doing it to destroy the ground but to purge the ground from thorns and briers.</u>**

Note: *This passage not only refers to saved people: v. 4 "were made partakers of the Holy Ghost" but also matured Christians. 6:1 "let us go on to perfection" & Heb.5:14 "But strong meat belongeth to them that are of full age"*

Note: *Bible examples:*

1) ***Saul:***
   a. Partaker of the Holy Spirit with great responsibilities.

   1Sam 10:6 *And* **<u>the Spirit of the LORD will come upon thee</u>**, *and thou shalt prophesy with them, and shalt be turned into another man.*

   1Sam 10:9 *And it was so, that when he had turned his back to go from Samuel,* **<u>God gave him another heart</u>**: *and all those signs came to pass that day.*

   1Sam 10:10 *And when they came thither to the hill, behold, a company of prophets met him; and*

the Spirit of God came upon him, and he prophesied among them.

1Sam 11:6 And **_the Spirit of God came upon Saul_** *when he heard those tidings, and his anger was kindled greatly.*

b. His falling away:

1Sam 13:9 *And Saul said, Bring hither a burnt offering to me, and peace offerings. And he offered the burnt offering.*

1Sam 13:12 *Therefore said I, The Philistines will come down now upon me to Gilgal, and I have not made supplication unto the LORD: I forced myself therefore, and offered a burnt offering.* **13** *And Samuel said to Saul, Thou hast done foolishly: thou hast not kept the commandment of the LORD thy God, which he commanded thee: for now would the LORD have established thy kingdom upon Israel for ever.*

1Sam 15:9 *But Saul and the people spared Agag, and the best of the sheep, and of the oxen, and of the fatlings, and the lambs, and all that was good, and would not utterly destroy them: but every thing that was vile and refuse, that they destroyed utterly.*

c. Impossible to restore him to being King again: *(He died)*

1Sam 15:11 It repenteth me that I have set up Saul to be king: for he is turned back from following me, and hath not performed my commandments. And it grieved Samuel; and he cried unto the LORD all night.

1Sam 16:1 And the LORD said unto Samuel, How long wilt thou mourn for Saul, seeing I have rejected him from reigning over Israel? fill thine horn with oil, and go, I will send thee to Jesse the Bethlehemite: for I have provided me a king among his sons.

*1Sam 28:19 Moreover the LORD will also deliver Israel with thee into the hand of the Philistines: and **to morrow shalt thou and thy sons be with me**: the LORD also shall deliver the host of Israel into the hand of the Philistines. 20 Then Saul fell straightway all along on the earth, and was sore afraid, because of the words of Samuel: and there was no strength in him; for he had eaten no bread all the day, nor all the night.*

2) *Moses*
   a. Partaker of the Holy Spirit with great responsibilities

   b. His falling away:

   (Num 20:8) Take the rod, and gather thou the assembly together, thou, and Aaron thy brother, and speak ye unto the rock before their eyes; and

it shall give forth his water, and thou shalt bring forth to them water out of the rock: so thou shalt give the congregation and their beasts drink.

(Num 20:10) And Moses and Aaron gathered the congregation together before the rock, and he said unto them, Hear now, ye rebels; must we fetch you water out of this rock? (Num 20:11) And Moses lifted up his hand, and with his rod he smote the rock twice: and the water came out abundantly, and the congregation drank, and their beasts also. (Num 20:12) And the LORD spake unto Moses and Aaron, Because ye believed me not, to sanctify me in the eyes of the children of Israel, therefore ye shall not bring this congregation into the land which I have given them.

c. His impossibility to lead children of Israel into promised land

*(Num 20:12) And the LORD spake unto Moses and Aaron, Because ye believed me not, to sanctify me in the eyes of the children of Israel, **therefore ye shall not bring this congregation into the land which I have given them.***

*(Deut 34:4) And the LORD said unto him, This is the land which I sware unto Abraham, unto Isaac, and unto Jacob, saying, I will give it unto thy seed: I have caused thee to see it with thine eyes, but **thou shalt not go over thither**.*

3) ***Man of God in I Kings 13***

a. Partaker of the Holy Spirit with great responsibilities.

b. His falling away:

(1Kgs 13:18) *He said unto him, I am a prophet also as thou art; and an angel spake unto me by the word of the LORD, saying, Bring him back with thee into thine house, that he may eat bread and drink water. But he lied unto him.* ***(1Kgs 13:19)*** <u>***So he went back with him, and did eat bread in his house, and drank water***</u>.

c. His impossibility to be restored (he was killed:

(1Kgs 13:21) *And he cried unto the man of God that came from Judah, saying, Thus saith the LORD, Forasmuch as thou hast disobeyed the mouth of the LORD, and hast not kept the commandment which the LORD thy God commanded thee,* ***(1Kgs 13:22)*** *But camest back, and hast eaten bread and drunk water in the place, of the which the LORD did say to thee, Eat no bread, and drink no water; thy carcase shall not come unto the sepulchre of thy fathers.* ***(1Kgs 13:23)*** *And it came to pass, after he had eaten bread, and after he had drunk, that he saddled for him the ass, to wit, for the prophet whom he had brought back.* ***(1Kgs 13:24)*** *And when he was gone, a lion met him by the way, and slew* *him: and his carcase was cast in the way, and the ass stood by it, the lion also stood by the carcase.*

*Note: These verses are referring to saved people who have matured enough to be entrusted with leadership positions and responsibilities (see **Heb. 5:14;6:1**) and have gotten into open sin and God removes them from that particular service with the warning that it is impossible to return to that position of service again. It is not a matter of forgiveness it is a matter of reaping what you sow. Unto much is given, much is required.*

Be Steadfast as Believers

Heb 6:9 But, beloved, we are persuaded better things of you, and **things that accompany salvation**, though we thus speak.

*Note: These things that are mentioned in verses **Heb. 5:11-14; 6:1-8** are not things that are required for salvation, they are all things that accompany salvation.*

God Will Reward Each Work

Heb 6:10 For God [is] not unrighteous to forget your work and labour of love, which ye have shewed toward his name, in that ye have ministered to the saints, and do minister.

Note: Remember the God we serve sees every kind deed and every effort in his service and all will be rewarded if they are of the right sort.

Diligence versus Laziness

Heb 6:11 And we desire that every one of you do **<u>shew the same diligence</u>** to the full assurance of hope unto the end:

Note: We need the same diligence that those who had gotten saved and matured before us and to continue the race set before us.

Heb 6:12 That ye **<u>be not slothful #3576</u>**, but followers of them who **<u>through faith and patience</u>** inherit the promises.

Note: "slothful" [#3576][2x][Heb. 5:11-dull]

Our laziness can be a great hindrance to our spiritual growth and progress.

Note: Two things that are necessary to receive and enjoy the promises of God are 'faith' and 'patience'.

The Promises of God are Sure as God

Heb 6:13 For when God made promise to Abraham, because he could swear by no <u>greater</u>, he sware by himself,

Heb 6:14 Saying, Surely blessing I will bless thee, and multiplying I will multiply thee.

*Note: C.R. **Gen 22:17** That **<u>in blessing I will bless thee, and in multiplying I will multiply thy seed</u>** as the stars of the heaven, and as the sand which is upon the sea shore; and thy seed shall possess the gate of his enemies;*

Receiving Promises through Patience

Heb 6:15 And so, <u>after he had patiently endured</u>, he obtained the promise.

Heb 6:16 For men verily swear by the greater: and an oath for confirmation [is] to them an end of all strife.

The Immutability of God's Counsel

Heb 6:17 Wherein God, willing more abundantly to shew unto the heirs of promise the immutability of his counsel, confirmed [it] by an oath:

Note: "immutablilty" [276][2x][v.17 &18][def. unchangeable]

When that which is perfect changes it is no longer perfect, so that is why God does not change and His Word does not change.

The Immutability of God's Word

Heb 6:18 That by two immutable things, in which [**it was] impossible for God to lie**, we might have a strong **consolation**, who have fled for refuge to lay hold upon the hope set before us:

Note: "consolation" #3874 (29x)(consolation 14, exhortation 8, comfort 6,intreaty)

Note: Jesus is our refuge.

Note: One of the reasons why we can claim God's promises is because God cannot lie and will not break His promises. Notice the following verse.

(Num 23:19) <u>**God is not a man, that he should lie; neither the son of man, that he should repent: hath he said, and shall he not do it? or hath he spoken, and shall he not make it good?**</u>

The Anchor of the Soul

Heb 6:19 Which [hope] we have as an anchor of the **soul**, both **sure** and **stedfast**, and which entereth into that within the veil;

Note: "soul" [5590][105x][soul-58; life-40; minds-3; heartily; heart; misc-2]

Note: "sure" [804][5x][certainly-2; certain; safe; sure]

Note: "stedfast" [949][9x][steadfast-4; sure-2; firm; of force; more sure-II Pet. 1:19]

Note: Jesus and His Word are the anchors of our soul.

The High Priest

Heb 6:20 Whither the forerunner is for us entered, [even] Jesus, made an high priest for ever after the order of Melchisedec.

Note: Jesus is high priest forever - after the order of Melchisedec. This refers to Jesus being both King and High Priest.

9

Hebrews Chapter 7

Melchisedec

Note: C.R. Psa. 110:4 [Gen. 14:18; Heb. 5:6, 10; 6:20; 7:1, 10, 11, 15

Heb. 7:21] verses on Melchisedec:

(Type of Royal Priesthood)

Heb 7:1 For this Melchisedec, **king** of Salem, **priest** of the most high God, who met Abraham returning from the slaughter of the kings, and blessed him;

(Tithed to By Abraham)

Heb 7:2 To whom also Abraham gave a <u>tenth</u> part of all; first being by interpretation King of righteousness, and after that also King of Salem, which is, King of peace;

Note: The definition of the word 'Melchisedec' is "king of righteousness".

Note: The definition of the word 'Salem' is "peace".

Note: "tenth" [1181][4 times][Heb. 7:2, 4, 8, 9-tithes]

Note: Tithing was practiced before the law and was taught during the law and cannot be disannulled by the law and the same is true with capital punishment.

(Melchisedec is a Type of Christ)

Heb 7:3 Without father, without mother, without descent, having neither beginning of days, nor end of life; but made like unto the Son of God; abideth a priest continually.

Note: There is no record of Melchisedec's father or mother or of his birth or his death. Like the Son of God or in other words, he is a type of Christ.

See v. 6 "he whose descent is not counted"

Note: "made like" [#871][1 time][def. to assimilate closely]

Heb 7:4 Now consider how great this man [was], unto whom even the patriarch Abraham gave the tenth of the spoils.

Note: "tenth" [#1181][4x][tithe-2; tenth part-1; tenth-1]

Note: Tithing was practiced before the law. Melchisedec was greater than Abraham and Jesus is greater than Melchisedec.

Heb 7:5 And verily they that are of the sons of Levi, who receive the office of the priesthood, have a commandment to take tithes of the people according to the law, that is, of their brethren, though they come out of the loins of Abraham:

Note: Jesus' priesthood is by an oath, but the Levitical priesthood was by the law.

Heb 7:6 But **<u>he whose descent is not counted</u>** from them received tithes of Abraham, and blessed him that had the promises.

Note: "descent is ... counted" [1075][1 time][def. reckon by genealogy]

So, Melchisedec's reference of no father or mother from verse 3 is not because he had no father or mother. It was simply because there was no record of the genealogy of his parents.

Heb 7:7 And without all contradiction the less is blessed of the better.

Note: Melchisedec is better than Abraham, and Jesus is better than Melchisedec.

Heb 7:8 And here men that die receive tithes; but there he [receiveth them], of whom it is witnessed that he liveth.

(Tithed to By Levi through Abraham)

Heb 7:9 And as I may so say, Levi also, who receiveth tithes, payed tithes in Abraham.

Note: "tithes" [1183][2][Heb. 7:6; 7:9]

Heb 7:10 For he was yet in the loins of his father, when Melchisedec met him.

Salvation has never come By the Law

Heb 7:11 If therefore perfection were by the Levitical priesthood, (for under it the people received the law,) what further need [was there] that another priest should rise after the order of Melchisedec, and not be called after the order of Aaron?

Heb 7:12 For the priesthood being changed, there is made of necessity a change also of the law.

Jesus' Human Side Came from Judah

Heb 7:13 For he of whom these things are spoken pertaineth to another tribe, of which no man gave attendance at the altar.

Heb 7:14 For [it is] evident that **our Lord sprang out of Juda**; of which tribe Moses spake nothing concerning priesthood.

Note: **Matt 1:3** *And* **Judas** *begat Phares and Zara of Thamar; and Phares begat Esrom; and Esrom begat Aram;*

Luke 3:33 *Which was the son of Aminadab, which was the son of Aram, which was the son of Esrom, which was the son of Phares,* **which was the son of Juda**,

Heb 7:15 And it is yet far more evident: for that after the similitude of Melchisedec there ariseth another priest,

Heb 7:16 Who is made, not after the law of a carnal commandment, but after the power of an endless life.

Note: The Levitical priesthood was temporary, but Jesus' priesthood is forever.

Heb 7:17 For he testifieth, Thou [art] a priest for ever after the order of Melchisedec.

Note: C.R. **Ps 110:4** *The LORD hath sworn, and will not repent, Thou art a priest for ever after the order of Melchizedek.*

Heb 7:18 For there is verily a **disannulling** of the commandment going before for the weakness and unprofitableness thereof.

Note: "disannulling" [#115][2x][Heb. 9:26 - put away]

The Law Could Not Save

Heb 7:19 For the law made nothing perfect, but the bringing in of a better hope [did]; by the which we draw nigh unto God.

Note: No one got saved by the law, nor could be saved by the law.

See the following passages:

Rom 3:20 *Therefore by the deeds of the law there shall no flesh be justified in his sight: for by the law is the knowledge of sin.*

Rom 3:28 *Therefore we conclude that a man is justified by faith without the deeds of the law.*

Gal 2:16 *Knowing that a man is not justified by the works of the law, but by the faith of Jesus Christ, even we have believed in Jesus Christ, that we might be justified by the faith of Christ, and not by the works of the law: for by the works of the law shall no flesh be justified.*

Gal 3:11 *But that no man is justified by the law in the sight of God, it is evident: for, The just shall live by faith.*

Gal 3:24 *Wherefore the law was our schoolmaster to bring us unto Christ, that we might be justified by faith.*

Heb 7:20 And inasmuch as not without an oath [he was made priest]:

Priesthood without an Oath versus Priesthood with an Oath

Heb 7:21 (For those priests were made without an oath; but this with an oath by him that said unto him, The Lord sware and will not repent, Thou [art] a priest for ever after the order of Melchisedec:)

*Note: C.R. **Ps 110:4** The LORD hath sworn, and will not repent, Thou art a priest for ever after the order of Melchizedek.*

Heb 7:22 By so much was Jesus made a surety of a better testament.

Temporary Priesthood versus Eternal Priesthood

Heb 7:23 And they truly were many priests, because they were not suffered to continue by reason of death:

Heb 7:24 But this [man], because he continueth ever, hath an unchangeable priesthood.

Salvation to the Uttermost

Heb 7:25 Wherefore he is able also to save them to the uttermost that come unto God by him, seeing he ever liveth to make intercession for them.

Note: No one can come to God but by Jesus.

John 14:6 *Jesus saith unto him, I am the way, the truth, and the life: no man cometh unto the Father, but by me.*

1Tim 2:5 *For there is one God, and one mediator between God and men, the man Christ Jesus;*

The Ultimate Priesthood

Heb 7:26 For such an high priest became us, [who is] holy, harmless, undefiled, separate from sinners, and made higher than the heavens;

Heb 7:27 Who needeth not daily, as those high priests, to offer up sacrifice, first for his own sins, and then for the people's: for this he did once, when he offered up himself.

Heb 7:28 For the law maketh men high priests which have infirmity; but the word of the oath, which was since the law, [maketh] the Son, who is **consecrated** for evermore.

Note: "consecrated" [#5048][24x][make perfect-12; perfect-4; finish-4; fulfil-2; be perfect; consecrate]

Note: In Hebrews Chapter 7 Jesus is compared to two types of priesthoods.

1) *The levitical priesthood*
2) *The priesthood of Melchisedec*
   In which Jesus is far better than both.

10

Hebrews Chapter 8

Summary of Jesus' High Priesthood
(The Priesthood is At the Right Hand of the Father)

Heb 8:1 Now of the things which we have spoken [this is] the sum: We have such an high priest, who is set on the right hand of the throne of the Majesty in the heavens;

(The Priesthood is In the True Tabernacle in Heaven)

Heb 8:2 A minister of the **<u>sanctuary</u>**, and of the true tabernacle, which **<u>the Lord pitched</u>**, and not man.

Note: "sanctuary" [#39][11x][Holiest of all-3; holy place-3; holiness; sanctuary-4]

(The Earthly Priesthood in Contrast with the Heavenly)

Heb 8:3 For every high priest is ordained to offer gifts and sacrifices: wherefore [it is] of necessity that this man have somewhat also to offer.

Heb 8:4 For if he were on earth, he should not be a priest, seeing that there are priests that offer gifts according to the law:

Heb 8:5 Who serve unto the example and shadow of heavenly things, as Moses was admonished of God when he was about to make the tabernacle: for, See, saith he, [that] thou make all things **according to the pattern shewed to thee in the mount**.

> Note: C.R. **Exod 25:9** *According to all that I shew thee,* **_after the pattern of the tabernacle, and the pattern of all the instruments thereof,_** *even so shall ye make it.*

> **Exod 25:40** *And look that thou make them* **_after their pattern, which was shewed thee in the mount._**

> Note: *The Levitical priesthood served in the model, but Jesus is serving in the real tabernacle in heaven.*

(The Priesthood with the Perfect Mediator)

Heb 8:6 But now hath he obtained a more excellent ministry, by how much also **he is the mediator of a better covenant**, which was established upon better promises.

Note: Jesus is the only mediator. See the following passages:

1Tim 2:5 *For there is one God,* **<u>and one mediator between God and men, the man Christ Jesus;</u>**

Heb 9:15 *And for this cause* **<u>he is the mediator of the new testament</u>**, *that by means of death, for the redemption of the transgressions that were under the first testament, they which are called might receive the promise of eternal inheritance.*

Heb 12:24 *And to* **<u>Jesus the mediator of the new covenant</u>**, *and to the blood of sprinkling, that speaketh better things than that of Abel.*

The First Covenant is Faultless

Heb 8:7 For if that first [covenant] had been faultless, then should no place have been sought for the second.

Heb 8:8 For finding fault with them, he saith, <u>Behold, the days come, saith the Lord, when I will make a new covenant with the house of Israel and with the house of Judah</u>:

Note: C.R. **Jer. 31:31-34** *goes with* **Heb 8:8-12**

Jer 31:31 *Behold, the days come, saith the LORD, that I will make a new covenant with the house of Israel, and with the house of Judah:*

Heb 8:9 <u>Not according to the covenant that I made with their fathers in the day when I took them by the hand to lead</u>

them out of the land of Egypt; because they continued not in my covenant, and I regarded them not, saith the Lord.

> *Note:* **Jer 31:32** *Not according to the covenant that I made with their fathers in the day that I took them by the hand to bring them out of the land of Egypt; which my covenant they brake, although I was an husband unto them, saith the LORD:*

Heb 8:10 For this [is] the covenant that I will make with the house of Israel after those days, saith the Lord; I will put my laws into their **mind**, and write them in their hearts: and I will be to them a God, and they shall be to me a people:

> *Note:* **Jer 31:33** *But this shall be the covenant that I will make with the house of Israel; After those days, saith the LORD, I will put my law in their* ***inward parts****, and write it in their hearts; and will be their God, and they shall be my people.*

Heb 8:11 And they shall not teach every man his neighbour, and every man his brother, saying, Know the Lord: for all shall know me, from the least to the greatest.

> *Note:* **Jer 31:34** *And they shall teach no more every man his neighbour, and every man his brother, saying, Know the LORD: for they shall all know me, from the least of them unto the greatest of them, saith the LORD**: for I will forgive their iniquity, and I will remember their sin no more.***

(The True Priesthood Brings Perfect Forgiveness)

Heb 8:12 For I will be merciful to their unrighteousness, and **their sins and their iniquities will I remember no more.**

Note: God remembering sin no more. See the following passages:

*Jer 31:34 And they shall teach no more every man his neighbour, and every man his brother, saying, Know the LORD: for they shall all know me, from the least of them unto the greatest of them, saith the LORD: for **I will forgive their iniquity, and I will remember their sin no more.***

*Isa 43:25 I, even I, am he that blotteth out thy transgressions for mine own sake, and **will not remember thy sins**.*

*When God forgives, he also forgets. Notice that **Hebrews 8:12** defines forgiveness as "**I will be merciful to their unrighteousness**." God will never convict you of confessed sin. Only Satan will try to weight you down with the guilt of the sins of your past even though we confessed the sins.*

The Old Covenant versus the New Covenant

Heb 8:13 In that he saith, A new [covenant], he hath made the first old. Now that which decayeth and waxeth old [is] ready to vanish away.

Note: "hath made old" [3822][4 times][Heb. 8:13 - that which decayeth;

[Heb. 1:11 - shall wax old - Lu. 12:33]

Note: "decayeth" [3822][4x][wax old-2; make old-1; decayeth-1]

Note: "waxeth old" [1095][2 times][John 21:18 - shalt be old]

11

Hebrews Chapter 9

The Earthly Tabernacle

Heb 9:1 Then verily the first [covenant] had also **ordinances** of **divine service**, and a worldly **sanctuary**.

Note: "ordinances" [#1345][10x][judgment-2; justification; ordinance-3; righteousness-4]

Note: "divine service" [#2999][5x][service - Rom. 12:1; Rom 9:4; Heb 9:12; 9:6)(9:1; divine service]

Note: "sanctuary" [#39][11x][sanctuary-4; holiest of all-3; holy place-3; holiest]

The First Part is the Sanctuary

Heb 9:2 For there was a tabernacle made; the first, wherein [was] the **candlestick**, and the **table**, and the **shewbread**; which is **called the sanctuary #39**.

Note: "the table, the candlestick, and the shewbread in the sanctuary"

*C.R. (**Exod 26:35**) And thou shalt set the **table** without the vail, and the **candlestick** over against the **table** on the side of the tabernacle <u>toward the south</u>: and thou shalt put the **table** on the <u>north side</u>.*

The Second Part is the Holiest of All

Heb 9:3 And **after the second veil**, the tabernacle which is called the **Holiest of all #39**;

*Note: "The veil" (**Heb 10:20**) By a new and living way, which he hath consecrated for us, through **the veil, that is to say, his flesh**;*

*C.R. (**Exod 26:31**) And thou shalt make a **vail** of blue, and purple, and scarlet, and fine twined linen of cunning work: with cherubims shall it be made: (**Exod 26:32**) And thou shalt hang it upon four pillars of shittim wood overlaid with gold: their hooks shall be of gold, upon the four sockets of silver. (**Exod 26:33**) And thou shalt hang up **the vail** under the taches, that thou mayest bring in thither within **the vail** the **ark of the testimony**: and the **vail** <u>shall divide unto you between the holy place and the most holy.</u> (**Exod 26:34**) And thou shalt put the **mercy seat** upon **the ark of the testimony** in the **most holy place**.*

The Ark and the Contents

Heb 9:4 Which had the **golden censer**, and the **ark of the covenant** overlaid round about with gold, wherein [was] <u>the golden pot that had manna</u>, and <u>Aaron's rod that budded</u>, and the <u>tables of the covenant</u>;

Note: "the ark"

C.R. (***Exod 25:10***) *And they shall make an **ark** of shittim wood:* <u>*two cubits and a half shall be the length thereof, and a cubit and a half the breadth thereof, and a cubit and a half the height thereof*</u>*.* (***Exod 25:11***) *And thou shalt overlay it with pure gold, within and without shalt thou overlay it, and shalt make upon it a crown of gold round about.* (***Exod 25:12***) *And thou shalt cast four rings of gold for it, and put them in the four corners thereof; and two rings shall be in the one side of it, and two rings in the other side of it.* (***Exod 25:13***) *And thou shalt make staves of shittim wood, and overlay them with gold.* (***Exod 25:14***) *And thou shalt put the staves into the rings by the sides of the **ark**, that the **ark** may be borne with them.* (***Exod 25:15***) *The staves shall be in the rings of the **ark**: they shall not be taken from it.* (***Exod 25:16***) *And thou shalt put into the **ark** the testimony which I shall give thee.*

The Mercy Seat

Heb 9:5 And over it the cherubims of glory shadowing the **mercyseat**; of which we cannot now speak particularly.

Note: "mercyseat" [#2435][2 times][propitiation - Rom. 3:25]

*C.R. (**Exod 25:17**) And thou shalt make a **mercy seat** of pure gold: two cubits and a half shall be the length thereof, and a cubit and a half the breadth thereof. (**Exod 25:18**) And thou shalt make two cherubims of gold, of beaten work shalt thou make them, in the two ends of the **mercy seat**. (**Exod 25:19**) And make one cherub on the one end, and the other cherub on the other end: even of the **mercy seat** shall ye make the cherubims on the two ends thereof. (**Exod 25:20**) And the cherubims shall stretch forth their wings on high, covering the **mercy seat** with their wings, and their faces shall look one to another; toward the **mercy seat** shall the faces of the cherubims be. (**Exod 25:21**) And thou shalt put the **mercy seat** above upon the ark; and in the ark thou shalt put the testimony that I shall give thee. (**Exod 25:22**) And there I will meet with thee, and I will commune with thee from above the **mercy seat**, from between the two cherubims which are upon the ark of the testimony, of all things which I will give thee in commandment unto the children of Israel.*

Heb 9:6 Now when these things were thus ordained, the priests went always into the **first tabernacle**, accomplishing the service [of God].

Note: "service" [#2999][5x][service (Rom. 12:1)-4; divine service]

The High Priest Once Every Year into the Holiest of All

Heb 9:7 But into the second [went] the high priest alone **once every year**, not without blood, which he offered for himself, and [for] the errors of the people:

> Note: C.R. **Lev 16:34** *And this shall be an everlasting statute unto you, to make an atonement for the children of Israel for all their sins* **once a year**. *And he did as the LORD commanded Moses.*

> **Exod 30:10** *And Aaron shall make an atonement upon the horns of it* **once in a year** *with the blood of the sin offering of atonements*: **once in the year** *shall he make atonement upon it throughout your generations: it is most holy unto the LORD.*

Heb 9:8 The Holy Ghost this signifying, that the way into the **holiest of all** was not yet made manifest, while as the first tabernacle was yet standing:

Heb 9:9 Which [was] a **figure** for the time then present, in which were offered both gifts and sacrifices, that could not make him that did the service perfect, as pertaining to the conscience;

> Note: "figure" [#3850][50x][figure-2; parables-46; comparison; proverb]

> Note: The Old Testament people were not saved by animal sacrifices.

> *They got saved just like we do today, only their faith looked foward to Jesus and His death on the cross and our faith looked back to the Jesus and His death on the cross. The animal sacrificing merely pictured the crucifixion that was to come and the sacrifice that Jesus would make on the cross.*

Heb 9:10 [Which stood] only in meats and drinks, and divers washings, and carnal ordinances, imposed [on them] until the time of reformation.

> *Note: "reformation" [#1357][1 time][def. to straighten thoroughly;*
>
> *The Messianic restoration; rectification]*

(The Priesthood of the Real Tabernacle)

Heb 9:11 But Christ being come an high priest of good things to come, by a greater and more perfect tabernacle, not made with hands, that is to say, not of this building;

> *Note: The Levitical priesthood served in the temporal model on earth, but Jesus serves in the permanent tabernacle in heaven forever.*

(The Priesthood with the Ultimate Sacrifice)

Heb 9:12 Neither by the blood of goats and calves, but **by his own blood he entered in once into the holy place, having obtained eternal redemption [for us].**

Note: The cardinal doctrine of the "blood atonement" has many cross references. Notice the passages below to name a few.

[Acts 20:28; Rom. 3:25; Rom. 5:9; Eph. 1:7; 2:13; Col. 1:14, 20; Heb. 9:12, 14, 22; Heb. 10:19; 13:12; II Pet. 1:2, 19; I John 1:7; Rev. 1:5; 5:9; Rev. 7:14; 12:11; Lev. 17:11]

Note: One of the reasons for Jesus' death is "to obtain eternal redemption for us".

Heb 9:13 For if the blood of bulls and of goats, and the ashes of an heifer sprinkling the unclean, sanctifieth to the purifying of the flesh:

The Trinity in the Plan of Redemption

Heb 9:14 How much more shall the **blood of Christ**, who through **the eternal Spirit** offered himself without spot to **God**, purge your conscience from dead works to serve the living God?

Note: The cardinal doctrine of the Trinity also has many cross references. Please see this author's book on "Cardinal Doctrines."

[Isa. 48:16; I Jn. 5:7; I Pet. 1:2; Mat. 28:19; I Pet. 3:18; Jn. 14:16

Jn. 14:26; 15:26; Eph. 2:18; Col. 2:2; I Thess. 3:11; Heb. 9:14]

Note: "purge" [#2511][30x][cleanse-16; make clean-5; clean-3; purge-3; purify-3]

Note: One of the immediate changes in a person when they get saved is a purged conscience to serve the living God.

The Perfect Mediator and Redemption

Heb 9:15 And for this cause he is the mediator of the new testament, that by means of death, for <u>the redemption of the transgressions [that were] under the first testament</u>, they which are called might receive the promise of eternal inheritance.

Note: "mediator" C.R. I Tim. 2:5; Heb. 8:6; 12:24

Note: "redemption" [629][10 times][deliverance; redemption-9]

Note: This verse makes it clear that Jesus died also for the Old Testament people showing us that salvation has always been the same.

When the Testament Comes into Force

Heb 9:16 For where a testament [is], there must also of necessity be the death of the testator.

Heb 9:17 For a testament [is] of force after men are dead: otherwise it is of no strength at all while the testator liveth.

Note: The New Testament did not go into effect until after Jesus died.

Somethings that took place after Jesus died and was resurrected.

Mat. 27:51 "<u>**the veil of the temple was rent in twain**</u>"

John 20:22; 7:38-39 <u>**Every believer was indwelt and sealed with the Holy Spirit**</u>.

*Note: The church started on resurrection day, Sunday, **John 20:19** where they were assembled and indwelt with the Holy Spirit and later were filled with the Holy Spirit at Pentecost. **Acts 2:4***

Dedicated by Blood

Heb 9:18 Whereupon neither the first [testament] was dedicated without blood.

Heb 9:19 For when Moses had spoken every precept to all the people according to the law, he took the blood of calves and of goats, with water, and scarlet wool, and hyssop, and sprinkled both the book, and all the people,

Heb 9:20 Saying, This [is] the blood of the testament which God hath enjoined unto you.

*Note: C.R. **Exod 24:8** And Moses took the blood, and sprinkled it on the people, and said, Behold **<u>the blood of</u>***

the covenant, which the LORD hath made with you concerning all these words.

Heb 9:21 Moreover he sprinkled with blood both the tabernacle, and all the vessels of the ministry.

The Fulfillment of Lev. 17:11

Heb 9:22 And almost all things are by the law purged with blood; and **without shedding of blood is no remission.**

Note: "remission" [859][17x][remission-9; forgiveness-6; deliverance; liberty]

*Note: See **Heb 9:12** for verses on the blood atonement.*

Lev 17:11 *For the life of the flesh is in the blood: and I have given it to you upon the altar to make an atonement for your souls: for **it is the blood that maketh an atonement for the soul.***

The Ultimate Sacrifice

Heb 9:23 [It was] therefore necessary that the patterns of things in the heavens should be purified with these; but the heavenly things themselves **with better sacrifices than these**.

Heb 9:24 For **Christ** is not entered into the holy places made with hands, [which are] the figures of the true; but into heaven itself, now to appear in the presence of God for us:

Note: The Levitical priesthood served in the temporary model on earth, but Jesus serves in the permanent tabernacle in heaven forever.

Heb 9:25 Nor yet that he should offer himself often, as the high priest entereth into the holy place every year with blood of others;

Heb 9:26 For then must he often have suffered since the foundation of the world: but now **once in the end of the world hath he appeared to put away sin by the sacrifice of himself.**

Note: Jesus also died on the cross to put away sin.

The Universal Appointment

Heb 9:27 And as it is **appointed** unto men once to die, but after this the judgment:

Note: "appointed" [#606][4x][laid up - Lu. 19:20; Col. 1:5; II Tim. 4:8]

Note: Death is the appointment that God has with mankind, which no man will be able to avoid, and then the judgment.

For the saved *- The Judgment Seat of Christ: Notice the references below:*

*(Rom 14:10) But why dost thou judge thy brother? or why dost thou set at nought thy brother? for **we shall all stand before the judgment seat of Christ**.*

*(2Cor 5:10) For **we must all appear before the judgment seat of Christ**; that every one may receive the things done in his body, according to that he hath done, whether it be good or bad.*

(1Cor 3:13) Every man's work shall be made manifest: for the day shall declare it, because it shall be revealed by fire; and the fire shall try every man's work of what sort it is. (1Cor 3:14) If any man's work abide which he hath built thereupon, he shall receive a reward. (1Cor 3:15) If any man's work shall be burned, he shall suffer loss: but he himself shall be saved; yet so as by fire.

For the lost - *The White Throne Judgment: See the following passage:*

*(Rev 20:11) And I saw **a great white throne**, and him that sat on it, from whose face the earth and the heaven fled away; and there was found no place for them. (Rev 20:12) And I saw the dead, small and great, stand before God; and the books were opened: and another book was opened, which is the book of life: and **the dead were judged out of those things which were written in the books, according to their works.** (Rev 20:13) And the sea gave up the dead which were in it; and death and hell delivered up the dead which were in them: and **they were judged every man according to their works**. (Rev 20:14) And death and hell were cast into the lake of fire. This is the*

*second death. **(Rev 20:15)** And whosoever was not found written in the book of life was cast into the lake of fire.*

Jesus Paid the Ultimate Sacrifice

Heb 9:28 So Christ was once offered to bear the sins of many; and unto them that look for him shall he appear the second time without sin unto salvation.

Note: Jesus died to bear the sins of many. [All is many. No one is left out.]

12

Hebrews Chapter 10

The Law and Animal Sacrifices Could Not Save

Heb 10:1 For the law having a shadow of good things to come, [and] not the very image of the things, <u>can never with those sacrifices which they offered year by year continually make the comers thereunto perfect</u>.

Note: The animal sacrificing could never save any one. We are saved by the sacrifice of Jesus Christ, his burial and his resurrection. (See v. 4) The animal sacrifice was just a shadow or picture of the real thing and not the real thing itself otherwise, v. 2, they would not need to stop.

Heb 10:2 For then would they not have ceased to be offered? because that the **worshippers** once purged should have had no more conscience of sins.

Note: "worshippers" [#3000][21x][shalt serve-17; worship - 4]

Note: More proof of the animal sacrifice not being able to save any one is its continual coming to sacrifice. It was just a picture of Jesus' sacrifice.

Heb 10:3 But in those [sacrifices there is] a remembrance again [made] of sins every year.

Heb 10:4 For [<u>it is</u>] <u>not possible that the blood of bulls and of goats should take away sins</u>.

Note: The animal sacrificing could never save anyone. We are saved by the sacrifice of Jesus Christ, his burial and his resurrection. (See v.1)

The O.T. believers looked forward to the cross, and we looked back to the cross.

The Sacrifice of Jesus Christ

Heb 10:5 Wherefore when he cometh into the world, he saith, Sacrifice and offering thou wouldest not, but a body hast thou prepared me:

Heb 10:6 In burnt offerings and [sacrifices] for sin thou hast had no pleasure.

Note: If animal sacrifices saved people there would be pleasure to God in them

Heb 10:7 Then said I, Lo, I come (in the volume of the book it is written of me,) to do thy will, O God.

Note: C.R. **Ps 40:6** *Sacrifice and offering thou didst not desire; mine ears hast thou opened: burnt offering and sin offering hast thou not required. 7 Then said I, Lo, I come: in the volume of the book it is written of me, 8 I delight to do thy will, O my God: yea, thy law is within my heart.*

Note: "volume" [2777][1 time][Heb.# 4039- 1 time][def. the entire roll]

Heb 10:8 Above when he said, Sacrifice and offering and burnt offerings and [offering] for sin thou wouldest not, neither hadst pleasure [therein]; which are offered by the law;

Heb 10:9 Then said he, Lo, I come to do thy will, O God. He taketh away the first, that he may establish the second.

Heb 10:10 By the which will <u>we are sanctified through the offering of the body of Jesus Christ once [for all].</u>

Note: Jesus died once for all by which we are sanctified. Jesus did not just die for the elect or just for those who will get saved. Jesus even died on the cross for those that refuse to be saved such as the false prophets. Note the following:

*(2Pet 2:1) But there were **false prophets** also among the people, even as there shall be **false teachers** among you, who privily shall bring in damnable heresies, **even denying the Lord that bought them**, and bring upon themselves swift destruction.*

Heb 10:11 And every priest standeth daily ministering and offering oftentimes the same **sacrifices, which can never take away sins:**

> *Note: The animal sacrificing could never save anyone. We are saved by the sacrifice of Jesus Christ, his burial and his ressurection. (See v.4)*

The One Sacrifice Forever

Heb 10:12 But this man, after he had offered **one sacrifice for sins forever**, sat down on the right hand of God;

> *Note: Jesus died on the cross to make the ultimate one time sacrifice for sins forever.*

Heb 10:13 From henceforth expecting till his enemies be made his footstool.

Heb 10:14 For by one offering he hath perfected forever them that are sanctified.

The Witness of God Is Greater

Heb 10:15 [Whereof] the Holy Ghost also is a witness to us: for after that he had said before,

> *Note: (**Rom 8:16**) The Spirit itself beareth witness with our spirit, that we are the children of God:*

(1John 5:9) *If we receive the witness of men,* **the witness of God is greater***: for this is the witness of God which he hath testified of his Son.*

Heb 10:16 This [is] the covenant that I will make with them after those days, saith the Lord, I will put my laws into their hearts, and in their minds will I write them;

> **C.R. (Jer 31:33)** <u>But this shall be the covenant that I will make with the house of Israel; After those days, saith the LORD, I will put my law in their inward parts, and write it in their hearts</u>; and will be their God, and they shall be my people. **(Jer 31:34)** And they shall teach no more every man his neighbour, and every man his brother, saying, Know the LORD: for they shall all know me, from the least of them unto the greatest of them, saith the LORD: for I will forgive their iniquity, <u>and I will remember their sin no more.</u>

Forgiven and Forgotten

Heb 10:17 And their sins and iniquities will I remember no more.

> *Note: C.R. Jer. 31:33-34 When God forgives sin he also forgets the sin.*

Heb 10:18 Now where remission of these [is, there is] no more offering for sin.

> *Note: "remission" [#859][17x][remission-9; forgiveness-6; deliverance; liberty]*

Boldness by the Blood

Heb 10:19 Having therefore, brethren, boldness to enter into the holiest by the blood of Jesus,

> *Note: The Blood Atonement [See **Heb. 9:12** for notes]*

Heb 10:20 By a new and living way, which he hath consecrated for us, through the veil, that is to say, his flesh;

> *Note: The veil of the temple is a type and representative of the flesh of Christ.*

The High Priest

Heb 10:21 And [having] an high priest over the house of God;

Blessed Assurance

Heb 10:22 Let us draw near with a true heart in full assurance of faith, <u>having our hearts sprinkled from an evil conscience</u>, and our bodies washed with pure water.

> *Note: **(Heb 9:14)** How much more shall the blood of Christ, who through the eternal Spirit offered himself without spot to God, **<u>purge your conscience from dead works</u>** to serve the living God?*

Heb 10:23 Let us hold fast the profession of [our] faith without wavering; (for he [is] faithful that promised;)

Note: God wants us to know that we are saved and not to be haunted with doubts. God's promise of heaven is as good as God's word.

Notice the following:

(1John 5:13) These things have I written unto you that believe on the name of the Son of God; that ye may know that ye have eternal life, and that ye may believe on the name of the Son of God.

(1John 2:25) And this is the promise that he hath promised us, even eternal life.

(John 10:27) My sheep hear my voice, and I know them, and they follow me: (John 10:28) And I give unto them eternal life; and they shall never perish, neither shall any man pluck them out of my hand. (John 10:29) My Father, which gave them me, is greater than all; and no man is able to pluck them out of my Father's hand.

(John 6:37) All that the Father giveth me shall come to me; and him that cometh to me I will in no wise cast out.

Pulling Together

Heb 10:24 And let us consider one another to provoke unto love and to good works:

Note: We must provoke one another for the good not the bad. This is part of the value of the assembling together.

Heb 10:25 Not forsaking the assembling of ourselves together, as the manner of some [is]; but exhorting [one another]: and so much the more, as ye see the day approaching.

Note: Yes, it is commanded of God for us to attend a bible believing church and to attend faithfully.

When God Brings Chastisement upon the Believers
Heb 10:26 For if **we** sin wilfully after that we have received the knowledge of the truth, there remaineth no more sacrifice for sins,

Note: With the pronouns 'we', the author is including himself with others which tells us he is referring to believers.

Note: There are only two different ways of sinning against God. There is sinning ignorantly and sinning willfully. The sin mentioned here is doing wrong despite knowing or having been taught better. "have received the knowledge of the truth" This is also called doing despite unto the Spirit of Grace. (v. 29)

Note: "No more sacrifice for sin" is referring to having no forgiveness for the practice of sin and is not referring to forgiveness for the penalty of sin. The practice of sinning ignorantly was covered but the practice of sinning willfully required confession of sin or else chastisement.

C.R. *(1John 1:9) If we confess our sins, he is faithful and just to forgive us our sins, and to cleanse us from all unrighteousness.*

Heb 10:27 But a certain fearful looking for of judgment and fiery indignation, which shall devour the adversaries.

Note: "adversaries" [5227][2 times][contrary-Col. 2:14]

Note: The judgment is chastisement for Christians and it is to purge the contrary character from our lives. See the following passages:

*(**Heb 12:5**) And ye have forgotten the exhortation which speaketh unto you as unto children, My son, despise not thou the chastening of the Lord, nor faint when thou art rebuked of him: (**Heb 12:6**) For whom the Lord loveth he chasteneth, and scourgeth every son whom he receiveth. (**Heb 12:7**) If ye endure chastening, God dealeth with you as with sons; for what son is he whom the father chasteneth not? (**Heb 12:8**) But if ye be without chastisement, whereof all are partakers, then are ye bastards, and not sons. (**Heb 12:9**) Furthermore we have had fathers of our flesh which corrected us, and we gave them reverence: shall we not much rather be in subjection unto the Father of spirits, and live? (**Heb 12:10**) For they verily for a few days chastened us after their own pleasure; but **he for our profit, that we might be partakers of his holiness**. (**Heb 12:11**) Now no chastening for the present seemeth to be joyous, but grievous: nevertheless **afterward it yieldeth the peaceable fruit of righteousness unto them which are exercised thereby**.*

> **(1Cor 11:32)** *But <u>when we are judged, we are chastened of the Lord, that we should not be condemned with the world</u>*.

Heb 10:28 He that despised Moses' law died without mercy under two or three witnesses:

> *Note: "despised" [114][16 times)[despise-8; reject-4; bring to nothing; frustrate; disannulleth; cast off]*

>> *Disobeying God's commands after we are taught better is doing despite unto the Spirit of grace. Any individual in the Old Testament times after being taught the commands of God and deliberately disobeying them was put to death.*

Heb 10:29 Of how much sorer punishment, suppose ye, shall he be thought worthy, who hath trodden under foot the Son of God, and hath counted the blood of the covenant, wherewith **he was sanctified**, an unholy thing, and hath **done despite unto the Spirit of grace?**

> *Note: "sorer" [5501][11 times][worse-10; sorer]*

> *Note: "hath trodden under foot" [2662][5 times][trample; tread; trodden down; tread underfoot-2]*

> *Note: The punishment is chastisement. See the following passage.*

(1Cor 11:32) But when we are judged, we are chastened of the Lord, that we should not be condemned with the world.

The punishment for the believer's willful sinning is chastisement. The punishment for the world of unbeliever's sinning is the condemnation to Hell.

Note: "he was sanctified" tells us the passage is referring to believers.

Disobeying God's commands after we are taught better is doing despite unto the Spirit of grace and inviting God's chastening hand.

Heb 10:30 For we know him that hath said, Vengeance [belongeth] unto me, I will recompense, saith the Lord. And again, <u>**The Lord shall judge his people**</u>.

Note: "recompense" [467][6 times]["repay"]

Note: "The Lord shall judge his people" is referring to Christians being chastised by God and is not a reference to unbelievers. See the following passages.

(Deut 32:36) For <u>***the LORD shall judge his people***</u>, *and repent himself for his servants, when he seeth that their power is gone, and there is none shut up, or left.*

(Ps 50:4) He shall call to the heavens from above, and to the earth, that <u>***he may judge his people.***</u>

> *(Ps 135:14)* *For **the LORD will judge his people**, and he will repent himself concerning his servants.*

> *Note: "Vengeance belongs to God" See the following passages.*

> *(Deut 32:35)* *To me belongeth vengeance, and recompence; their foot shall slide in due time: for the day of their calamity is at hand, and the things that shall come upon them make haste.*

> *(Ps 94:1)* *O LORD God, to whom vengeance belongeth; O God, to whom vengeance belongeth, shew thyself.*

> *(Rom 12:19)* *Dearly beloved, avenge not yourselves, but rather give place unto wrath: for it is written, Vengeance is mine; I will repay, saith the Lord.*

Heb 10:31 [It is] a fearful thing to fall into the hands of the living God.

> *Note: No believer comes back from God's woodshed laughing.*

Looking Back on the Past Sufferings

Heb 10:32 But call to remembrance the former days, in which, after ye were illuminated, ye endured a great fight of afflictions;

> *Note: "illuminated" [5461][11 times][doth give light-2; bring to light-2; lighten-2; enlighten-2; light; illuminated; to make see]*

Heb 10:33 Partly, whilst ye were made a gazingstock both by reproaches and afflictions; and partly, whilst ye became companions of them that were so used.

Note: "made a gazingstock" [2301][1 time][rt.# 2302- theatre or spectacle]

Note: "companions of them that were so used" We are in God company when we suffer persecutions and afflictions for the cause of Christ.

Your own Suffering Helps us to Have Compassion on Others Who Are Now Suffering or Receive Persecutions

Heb 10:34 For ye had compassion of me in my bonds, and took joyfully the spoiling of your goods, knowing in yourselves that ye have in heaven a better and an enduring substance.

Note: "compassion" [4834][2 times][Heb. 4:15- touched with the feeling of]

Note: "bonds" [1199][20 times][bond-15; bands-3; chains - Jude 6; string]

Note: Looking forward to what is waiting for us in heaven helps us get through the trials and afflictions down here.

Stand Fast in the Faith

Heb 10:35 Cast not away therefore your confidence, which hath great recompence of reward.

Note: Keep your confidence and faith in God where it belongs.

(Ps 118:8) It is better to trust in the LORD than to put confidence in man.

(Ps 118:9) It is better to trust in the LORD than to put confidence in princes.

Patience for God's Promises

Heb 10:36 For ye have need of patience, that, after ye have done the will of God, ye might receive the promise.

Note: A child of God's lack of patience can hinder him from receiving the promises of God.

Jesus Is Sure To Come

Heb 10:37 For yet **a little while**, and he that shall come will come, and will not tarry.

Note: "tarry" [5549][5 times][delayeth-2; tarry-2; tarry so long]

Note: "a little while" Jesus' coming is always closer than it has ever been.

True Faith in Christ Lasts

Heb 10:38 Now the just shall live by faith: but if [any man] draw back, my soul shall have no pleasure in him.

Heb 10:39 But we are not of them who draw back unto perdition; but of **them that believe to the saving of the soul.**

Note: "perdition" [684][20 times][[perdition-8; destruction-5; waste-2; damnable; to die; perish; damnation; pernicious]

Note: A test of true faith is time. See the following passage.

(1John 2:19) They went out from us, but they were not of us; for if they had been of us, they would no doubt have continued with us: but they went out, that they might be made manifest that they were not all of us.

Temporary faith is a mere consideration. True faith is a dependence on Christ only for salvation. Temporary faith only gives false security. True faith gives eternal security. Temporary faith only temporarily changes your mind. True faith changes your mind and then progressively God will change your life.

If a person is genuinely saved, as a result, they will "hold the beginning of their confidence steadfast unto the end." They will not be looking for anything else to save them but Jesus. Genuine faith brings genuine salvation. A true test of genuine salvation is what we are depending on to get us to heaven through time. If it is a temporary belief, it is not a genuine faith and we will have a tendency to add to our temporary belief, works and deeds that we do to help get us into heaven. It is a mere consideration. Remember salvation is instant the moment you trust Christ as Savior. However, when you put your faith in Christ to be your Savior, not only are you given eternal life immediately, you will not be looking for anything else to save you.

13

Hebrews Chapter 11

**(The Hebrews Hall Of Faith)
Definition of Faith**

Heb 11:1 Now <u>**faith**</u> is the substance *(confidence)* of things hoped for, the evidence *(conviction)* of things not seen.

Note: "substance" [5287][5 times][confident; confidence-2; substance; person]

Note: For the "person" used with this Greek # 5287 in **Heb. 1:3** *is Jesus.*

(Heb 1:3) *Who being the brightness of his glory, and the express image of his* <u>***person***</u> ***#5287***, *and upholding all things by the word of his power, when he had by himself purged our sins, sat down on the right hand of the Majesty on high;*

Gerald McDaniel

Note: "evidence" [1650][2 times][reproof - II Tim. 3:16]

[rt. # 1651][17 times][being convicted; convinceth; rebuke]

Examples of True Faith

Heb 11:2 For **by it** the elders obtained a good report.

Note: "obtained a good report" [3140][79 times][bear wotmess-25; testify-19; bear record-13; witness-5; be a witness-2; give testimony-2; have a good report-2; misc.-11]

Heb 11:3 Through faith we understand that the worlds were framed by the word of God, so that things which are seen were not made of things which do appear.

Note: "framed" [2675][13 times][perfect-2; makeperfect-2; mend-2; be perfect-2; fit; frame; prepare; restore; perfectly joined together]

Note: Creation is taught by the Word of God and is accepted by faith knowing that evolution is a big lie. The infidels try to use the things that are seen to prove evolution and ignore the fact that life cannot come from dead matter. All life has to come from life and the source of life is God.

The Faith of Abel

Heb 11:4 By faith Abel offered unto God a more excellent sacrifice than Cain, by which he obtained witness that he was righteous, God testifying of his gifts: and by it he being dead yet speaketh.

132

Note: (Gen 4:3) And in process of time it came to pass, that Cain brought of the fruit of the ground an offering unto the LORD. (Gen 4:4) And Abel, he also brought of the firstlings of his flock and of the fat thereof. And the LORD had respect unto Abel and to his offering: (Gen 4:5) But unto Cain and to his offering he had not respect. And Cain was very wroth, and his countenance fell. (Gen 4:6) And the LORD said unto Cain, Why art thou wroth? and why is thy countenance fallen? (Gen 4:7) If thou doest well, shalt thou not be accepted? and if thou doest not well, sin lieth at the door. And unto thee shall be his desire, and thou shalt rule over him. (Gen 4:8) And Cain talked with Abel his brother: and it came to pass, when they were in the field, that Cain rose up against Abel his brother, and slew him. (Gen 4:9) And the LORD said unto Cain, Where is Abel thy brother? And he said, I know not: Am I my brother's keeper? (Gen 4:10) And he said, What hast thou done? the voice of thy brother's blood crieth unto me from the ground.

Note: Because Abel was saved, he offered a more excellent sacrifice. It was not that he was saved because he offered a more excellent sacrifice. The proper sacrifice given was a result of his salvation not the cause of his salvation. The sacrifice must be a blood offering and not the fruit of the ground. Notice the following passage.

*(Lev 17:11) For the life of the flesh is in the blood: and I have given it to you upon the altar to make an atonement for your souls: for **it is the blood that maketh an atonement for the soul.***

The Faith of Enoch

Heb 11:5 <u>By faith</u> Enoch was translated that he should not see death; and was not found, because God had translated *(removed)* him: for before his translation *(removing)* he had this testimony, that he pleased God.

> *Note: "translated" [3346][6][were carried; removed; being changed; turn; translated-2]*

> *Note: "translation" [3331][3 times][change; removing; translation]*

> *C.R.* *(Gen 5:22)* *And Enoch walked with God after he begat Methuselah three hundred years, and begat sons and daughters:* *(Gen 5:23)* *And all the days of Enoch were three hundred sixty and five years:* *(Gen 5:24)* *And Enoch walked with God: and he was not; for God took him.*

Without Faith It is Impossible to Please God

Heb 11:6 But without **faith** [it is] impossible to please [him]: for he that cometh to God must believe that he is, and [that] he is a rewarder of them that diligently seek him.

> *Note: You cannot approach God like a test tube, "he that cometh to God must believe that he is". You can only approach God by faith and true faith comes only by hearing the word of God.* *(Rom. 10:17)* *The closer you get to God, the more rewarding it will be.*

(Rom 10:17) *So then faith cometh by hearing, and hearing by the word of God.*

The Faith of Noah

Heb 11:7 <u>**By faith**</u> Noah, being warned of God of things not seen as yet, moved with fear, prepared an ark to the saving of his house; by the which he condemned the world, and became heir of the <u>**righteousness which is by faith**</u>.

Note: C.R. Gen. Chapter 6-8

Note: In the world that we live in, there are two types of righteousness. There is the righteousness by faith and the righteousness by the law. The righteousness by faith depends on what Jesus did on the cross to get them to heaven. The righteousness by the law depends on what people do to get them to heaven.

Notice the following versus on the "righteousness by faith."

(Rom 3:21) *But now* <u>***the righteousness of God without the law***</u> *is manifested, being witnessed by the law and the prophets;* *(Rom 3:22)* *Even* <u>***the righteousness of God which is by faith of Jesus Christ unto all and upon all them that believe***</u>*: for there is no difference:*

(Rom 4:5) *But* <u>***to him that worketh not, but believeth on him that justifieth the ungodly, his faith is counted for righteousness***</u>.

(Rom 4:9) *Cometh this blessedness then upon the circumcision only, or upon the uncircumcision also? for we say that **faith was reckoned to Abraham for righteousness.***

(Rom 4:13) *For the promise, that he should be the heir of the world, was not to Abraham, or to his seed, through the law, but through **the righteousness of faith.***

(Rom 9:30) *What shall we say then? That the Gentiles, which followed not after righteousness, have attained to righteousness, even **the righteousness which is of faith.***

(Rom 10:6) *But **the righteousness which is of faith** speaketh on this wise, Say not in thine heart, Who shall ascend into heaven? (that is, to bring Christ down from above:)* *(Rom 10:7)* *Or, Who shall descend into the deep? (that is, to bring up Christ again from the dead.)* *(Rom 10:8)* *But what saith it? The word is nigh thee, even in thy mouth, and in thy heart: that is, the word of faith, which we preach;* *(Rom 10:9)* *That if thou shalt confess with thy mouth the Lord Jesus, and shalt believe in thine heart that God hath raised him from the dead, thou shalt be saved.* *(Rom 10:10)* *For **with the heart man believeth unto righteousness**; and with the mouth confession is made unto salvation.*

(Gal 5:5) *For we through the Spirit wait for the hope of **righteousness by faith**.*

(Phil 3:9) *And be found in him, **not having mine own righteousness, which is of the law**, **but that which is***

through the faith of Christ, the righteousness which is of God by faith:

Now, notice the passages that refer to the "righteousness by law."

(Deut 6:25) *And* **_it shall be our righteousness, if we observe to do all these commandments before the LORD our God, as he hath commanded us_**.

(Isa 64:6) *But we are all as an unclean thing, and* **_all our righteousnesses are as filthy rags_**; *and we all do fade as a leaf; and our iniquities, like the wind, have taken us away.*

(Rom 8:4) *That* **_the righteousness of the law_** *might be fulfilled in us, who walk not after the flesh, but after the Spirit.*

(Rom 9:31) *But Israel, which followed after* **_the law of righteousness_**, *hath not attained to the* **_law of righteousness_**.

(Rom 10:4) *For Christ is the end of* **_the law for righteousness_** *to every one that believeth.* **(Rom 10:5)** *For Moses describeth* **_the righteousness which is of the law_**, *That the man which doeth those things shall live by them.*

(Gal 2:21) *I do not frustrate the grace of God:* **_for if righteousness come by the law, then Christ is dead in vain._**

*(Gal 3:21) Is the law then against the promises of God? God forbid: for **if there had been a law given which could have given life, verily righteousness should have been by the law.***

Righteousness by faith is what saves you by relying on the work that Jesus did on the cross to get you to heaven. Righteousness by law is what gives you false security and relying on your own works and deeds to get you to heaven is proof that you are not relying on what Jesus did to get you to heaven which means you will not go to heaven.

The Faith of Abraham

Heb 11:8 <u>By faith</u> Abraham, when he was called to go out into a place which he should after receive for an inheritance, obeyed; and <u>he went out, not knowing whither he went</u>.

*Note: C.R. **(Gen 12:1)** Now the LORD had said unto Abram, Get thee out of thy country, and from thy kindred, and from thy father's house, **<u>unto a land that I will shew thee:</u> (Gen 12:2)** And I will make of thee a great nation, and I will bless thee, and make thy name great; and thou shalt be a blessing: **(Gen 12:3)** And I will bless them that bless thee, and curse him that curseth thee: and in thee shall all families of the earth be blessed. **(Gen 12:4)** So Abram departed, as the LORD had spoken unto him; and Lot went with him: and Abram was seventy and five years old when he departed out of Haran.*

Note: This does not mean that Abraham was guessing on where he was going neither was Abraham wondering around. It means that God was leading Abraham where he had never been before. Remember, living by faith is following God's instructions (the Bible) and not guessing.

Heb 11:9 <u>**By faith**</u> he sojourned in the land of promise, as [in] a strange country, dwelling in tabernacles with Isaac and Jacob, the heirs with him of the same promise:

Heb 11:10 For <u>**he looked for a city which hath foundations, whose builder and maker [is] God.**</u>

Note: See Rev. 21. The city Abraham is looking for is the New Jerusalem.

The Faith of Sara

Heb 11:11 <u>**Through faith**</u> also Sara herself received strength to conceive seed, and was delivered of a child when she was past age, because she judged him faithful who had promised.

*Note: C.R. **(Gen 17:19)** And God said, Sarah thy wife shall bear thee a son indeed; and thou shalt call his name Isaac: and I will establish my covenant with him for an everlasting covenant, and with his seed after him.*

***(Gen 21:1)** And the LORD visited Sarah as he had said, and the LORD did unto Sarah as he had spoken. **(Gen 21:2)** For Sarah conceived, and bare Abraham a son in his old age, at the set time of which God had spoken to him. **(Gen 21:3)** And Abraham called the name of his son that was born unto him, whom Sarah bare to him, Isaac. **(Gen 21:4)** And Abraham circumcised his son Isaac being eight* *days old, as God had commanded him. **(Gen 21:5)** And Abraham was an hundred years old, when his son Isaac was born unto him.*

Note: Faith is simply believing God will do what he promised. You are taking God at His Word.

Heb 11:12 Therefore sprang there even of one, and him as good as dead, [so many] as the stars of the sky in multitude, and as the sand which is by the sea shore innumerable.

*Note: C.R. **(Gen 22:17)** That in blessing I will bless thee, and in multiplying I will multiply thy seed as the stars of the heaven, and as the sand which is upon the sea shore; and thy seed shall possess the gate of his enemies;*

Dying in Faith

Heb 11:13 These all **died in faith**, not having received the promises, but having **seen** them afar off, and were **persuaded** of [them], and **embraced** [them], and confessed that they were strangers and pilgrims on the earth.

Note: "persuaded" [3982][55][trusted-8; persuade-22; shall assure; confidence-8; obey-7; believe-3; misc-6]

Note: A step by step procedure on how to receive the promises of God:

a. See or recognize the promise in the Bible

b. Believe the promise or accept the promise as true.

c. Embrace the promise or take the promise personal and claim it for your own.

Faith Looking Forward to Heaven

Heb 11:14 For they that say such things declare plainly that <u>**they seek a country**</u>.

The Danger of Looking Back

Heb 11:15 And truly, <u>**if they had been mindful of that [country] from whence they came out**</u>, they might have had opportunity to have returned.

*Note: See **(Phil 2:5)** Let this mind be in you, which was also in Christ Jesus:*

(Phil 4:8) *Finally, brethren, whatsoever things are true, whatsoever things are honest, whatsoever things are just, whatsoever things are pure, whatsoever things are lovely, whatsoever things are of good report; if there be any virtue, and if there be any praise, think on these things.*

(2Cor 10:5) *Casting down imaginations, and every high thing that exalteth itself against the knowledge of God, and* <u>***bringing into captivity every thought to the obedience of Christ;***</u>

If our mind is dwelling on the old world and the old worldly ways, we will attempt to return to the old world and the old sinful lifestyle.

(Prov 23:7) For __as he thinketh in his heart, so is he__: Eat and drink, saith he to thee; but his heart is not with thee.

Faith Looking Forward to Heaven

Heb 11:16 But now they desire a better [country], that is, an heavenly: wherefore God is not ashamed to be called their God: for **he hath prepared for them a city**.

Note: (__John 14:2__) In my Father's house are many mansions: if it were not so, I would have told you. __I go to prepare a place for you.__ (__John 14:3__) And if I go and prepare a place for you, I will come again, and receive you unto myself; that where I am, there ye may be also.

The Faith of Abraham

Heb 11:17 **By faith** Abraham, when he was tried, offered up Isaac: and he that had received the promises offered up **his only begotten [son]**,

Note: C.R. (__Gen 22:1__) And it came to pass after these things, that God did tempt Abraham, and said unto him, Abraham: and he said, Behold, here I am. (__Gen 22:2__) And he said, __Take now thy son, thine only son Isaac__, whom thou lovest, and get thee into the land of Moriah; and offer him there for a burnt offering upon one of the mountains which I will tell thee of. (__Gen 22:3__) And Abraham rose up early in the morning, and saddled his ass, and took two of his young men with him, and Isaac his son, and clave the wood for the burnt offering, and rose up, and went unto the place of which God had told him. (Gen 22:4) Then on the third day Abraham lifted up his eyes, and saw the place afar off. (Gen 22:5) And Abraham said unto his young men, Abide ye here with the ass; and I and the lad will go yonder and worship, and come again to you.

Note: It is worth noting the last part of the statement in verse 5. "I and the lad will go yonder and worship, and come again to you." This part of the sentence has a compound subject. (I and the lad) The verbs are (will go; worship; come). Abraham knew that the lad would return with him. Otherwise, you would have to break the compound subject and say, "I will come again to you."

Note: "the only begotton son"

*(John 1:14) And the Word was made flesh, and dwelt among us, (and we beheld his glory, the glory as of **the only begotten of the Father**,) full of grace and truth.*

*(John 1:18) No man hath seen God at any time; **the only begotten Son**, which is in the bosom of the Father, he hath declared him.*

*(John 3:16) For God so loved the world, that he gave **his only begotten Son**, that whosoever believeth in him should not perish, but have everlasting life.*

*(John 3:18) He that believeth on him is not condemned: but he that believeth not is condemned already, because he hath not believed in the name of **the only begotten Son of God.***

*(1John 4:9) In this was manifested the love of God toward us, because that God sent **his only begotten Son** into the world, that we might live through him.*

Isaac was a type of Christ.

Heb 11:18 Of whom it was said, That **in Isaac shall thy seed be called**:

*Note: C.R. **(Gen 21:12)** And God said unto Abraham, Let it not be grievous in thy sight because of the lad, and because of thy bondwoman; in all that Sarah hath said unto thee, hearken unto her voice; for **in Isaac shall thy seed be called**.*

Heb 11:19 Accounting that God [was] able to raise [him] up, even from the dead; from whence also he received him in a figure.

Note: "figure" [3850][50 times][parable-46; comparison; proverb; figure-2]

Note: Abraham knew that God was able to raise up Isaac from the dead, if God allowed him to go through with his request. Sometimes God will lead you a certain way, just to see if you are willing to do it.

Note: God told him to do it. So, he believed God and did it. The act of Abraham offering up his son as a sacrifice in itself is not a test of faith. Many heathens sacrifice their own children to idols every day, but God asked a believer to do it to see if he would obey God. Abraham was tested to prove which he loved most, Isaac or God.

The Faith of Isaac

Heb 11:20 <u>By faith</u> Isaac blessed Jacob and Esau concerning things to come.

The Blessing of Jacob

(Gen 27:28) Therefore God give thee of the dew of heaven, and the fatness of the earth, and plenty of corn and wine: (Gen 27:29) Let people serve thee, and nations bow down to thee: be lord over thy brethren, and let thy mother's sons bow down to thee: cursed be every one that curseth thee, and blessed be he that blesseth thee.

The Blessing of Esau

(Gen 27:39) And Isaac his father answered and said unto him, Behold, thy dwelling shall be the fatness of the earth, and of the dew of heaven from above; (Gen 27:40) And by thy sword shalt thou live, and shalt serve thy brother; and it shall come to pass when thou shalt have the dominion, that thou shalt break his yoke from off thy neck.

The Faith of Jacob

Heb 11:21 <u>By faith</u> Jacob, when he was a dying, blessed both the sons of Joseph; and worshipped, [leaning] upon the top of his staff.

*Note: C.R. **(Gen 48:14)** And Israel stretched out his right hand, and laid it upon Ephraim's head, who was the younger, and his left hand upon Manasseh's head, guiding his hands wittingly; for Manasseh was the firstborn. **(Gen 48:15)** And he blessed Joseph, and said, God, before whom my fathers Abraham and Isaac did walk, the God which fed me all my life long unto this day, **(Gen 48:16)** <u>**The Angel which redeemed me from all evil, bless the lads; and let my name be named on them, and the name of my fathers Abraham and Isaac; and let them grow into a multitude in the midst of the earth.**</u>*

The Faith of Joseph

Heb 11:22 <u>**By faith**</u> Joseph, when he died, made mention of the departing of the children of Israel; and gave commandment concerning his bones.

*Note: C.R. **(Gen 50:24)** And Joseph said unto his brethren, I die: and God will surely visit you, and bring you out of this land unto the land which he sware to Abraham, to Isaac, and to Jacob. **(Gen 50:25)** And Joseph took an oath of the children of Israel, saying, God will surely visit you, and <u>**ye shall carry up my bones from hence.**</u> **(Gen 50:26)** So Joseph died, being an hundred and ten years old: and they embalmed him, and he was put in a coffin in Egypt.*

The Faith of Moses' Parents

Heb 11:23 <u>**By faith**</u> Moses, when he was born, was hid three months of his parents, because they saw [he was] a proper child; and they were not afraid of the king's commandment.

Note: God told them to do it. So, they believed God and did it.

Note: "proper" [791][2x][fair - Acts 7:20]

Note: C.R. ***(Exod 2:1)*** *And there went a man of the house of Levi, and took to wife a daughter of Levi.* ***(Exod 2:2)*** *And the woman conceived, and bare a son: and when she saw him that he was a goodly child, she hid him three months.* ***(Exod 2:3)*** *And when she could not longer hide him, she took for him an ark of bulrushes, and daubed it with slime and with pitch, and put the child therein; and she laid it in the flags by the river's brink.*

Note: We are to submit ourselves unto the authorities that be until they conflict with God's word. Notice the following passages.

(Acts 4:19) *But Peter and John answered and said unto them,* <u>***Whether it be right in the sight of God to hearken unto you more than unto God***</u>*, judge ye.* ***(Acts 4:20)*** *For we cannot but speak the things which we have seen and heard.*

(Acts 5:29) *Then Peter and the other apostles answered and said,* <u>***We ought to obey God rather than men.***</u>

The Faith of Moses

Heb 11:24 <u>**By faith**</u> Moses, when he was come to years, refused to be called the son of Pharaoh's daughter;

> *Note: C.R.* **(Exod 2:11)** *And it came to pass in those days, when Moses was grown, that he went out unto his brethren, and looked on their burdens: and he spied an Egyptian smiting an Hebrew, one of his brethren.* **(Exod 2:12)** *And he looked this way and that way, and when he saw that there was no man, he slew the Egyptian, and hid him in the sand.* **(Exod 2:13)** *And when he went out the second day, behold, two men of the Hebrews strove together: and he said to him that did the wrong, Wherefore smitest thou thy fellow?* **(Exod 2:14)** *And he said, Who made thee a prince and a judge over us? intendest thou to kill me, as thou killedst the Egyptian? And Moses feared, and said, Surely this thing is known.* **(Exod 2:15)** *Now when Pharaoh heard this thing, he sought to slay Moses. But Moses fled from the face of Pharaoh, and dwelt in the land of Midian: and he sat down by a well.*

The Faith of Moses

Heb 11:25 Choosing rather to suffer affliction with the people of God, than to enjoy the pleasures of sin for a season;

> *Note: Sin has pleasure for a season but only for a season.*

> *Sin thrills* **(Heb. 11:25)** *Sin chills* **(Matt. 24:12)** *Sin kills* **(Rom. 6:23)**

Heb 11:26 Esteeming the reproach of Christ greater riches than the treasures in Egypt: for he had respect unto the recompence of the reward.

Note: Faith will let us see the reward ahead in heaven clearer than the riches the world has to offer in this life.

Heb 11:27 <u>By faith</u> he forsook Egypt, not fearing the wrath of the king: for he endured, as <u>**seeing him who is invisible**</u>.

Note: By faith we can see him who is invisible.

> ***(Rom 10:17)*** *So then faith cometh by hearing, and hearing by the word of God.*

Note: God told him to do it. So, he believed God and did it.

Heb 11:28 <u>Through faith</u> he kept **<u>the passover</u>**, and the sprinkling of blood, lest he that destroyed the firstborn should touch them.

The Passover

*Note: C.R. **(Exod 12:3)** Speak ye unto all the congregation of Israel, saying, In the tenth day of this month <u>they shall take to them every man a lamb, according to the house of their fathers, a lamb for an house</u>: **(Exod 12:4)** And if the household be too little for the lamb, let him and his neighbour next unto his house take it according to the number of the souls; every man according to his eating shall make your count for the lamb. **(Exod 12:5)** <u>Your lamb</u>*

shall be without blemish, a male of the first year: ye shall take it out from the sheep, or from the goats: (**Exod 12:6**) *And ye shall keep it up until the fourteenth day of the same month: and the whole assembly of the congregation of Israel shall kill it in the evening.* (**Exod 12:7**) *And they shall take of the blood, and strike it on the two side posts and on the upper door post of the houses, wherein they shall eat it.* (**Exod 12:8**) *And they shall eat the flesh in that night, roast with fire, and unleavened bread; and with bitter herbs they shall eat it.* (**Exod 12:9**) *Eat not of it raw, nor sodden at all with water, but roast with fire; his head with his legs, and with the purtenance thereof.* (**Exod 12:10**) *And ye shall let nothing of it remain until the morning; and that which remaineth of it until the morning ye shall burn with fire.* (**Exod 12:11**) *And thus shall ye eat it; with your loins girded, your shoes on your feet, and your staff in your hand; and ye shall eat it in haste:* **it is the LORD'S passover**.

(**Exod 12:23**) *For the LORD will pass through to smite the Egyptians; and* **when he seeth the blood** *upon the lintel, and on the two side posts***, the LORD will pass over the door, and will not suffer the destroyer to come in unto your houses to smite you**. (**Exod 12:24**) *And ye shall observe this thing for an ordinance to thee and to thy sons for ever.* (**Exod 12:25**) *And it shall come to pass, when ye be come to the land which the LORD will give you, according as he hath promised, that ye shall keep this service.* (**Exod 12:26**) *And it shall come to pass, when your children shall say unto you, What mean ye by this service?* (**Exod 12:27**) *That ye shall say,* **It is the sacrifice of the**

LORD'S _passover_, *who passed over the houses of the children of Israel in Egypt, when he smote the Egyptians, and delivered our houses. And the people bowed the head and worshipped.*

Note: God told him to do it. So, he believed God and did it.

The Faith to Go through the Red Sea

Heb 11:29 By faith they passed through the Red sea **as by dry [land]:** which the Egyptians assaying to do were drowned.

Note: Countless times in the Bible we are told that the children of Israel crossed the Red sea as by dry land, and still we hear from infidels who claim to believe the Bible say they crossed through shallow waters.

Note: Notice the following passages.

*(**Exod 15:19**) For the horse of Pharaoh went in with his chariots and with his horsemen into the sea, and the LORD brought again the waters of the sea upon them; but **the children of Israel went on dry land in the midst of the sea**.*

*(**Neh 9:11**) And thou didst divide the sea before them, so that they **went through the midst of the sea on the dry land**; and their persecutors thou threwest into the deeps, as a stone into the mighty waters.*

(Ps 66:6) <u>**He turned the sea into dry land: they went**</u> <u>**through the flood on foot**</u>*: there did we rejoice in him.*

(Exod 14:21) *And Moses stretched out his hand over the sea; and the LORD caused the sea to go back by a strong east wind all that night, and* <u>**made the sea dry land**</u>*, and the waters were divided.* *(Exod 14:22)* *And the children of Israel went into the midst of the sea* <u>**upon the**</u> <u>**dry ground**</u>*: and the waters were a wall unto them on their right hand, and on their left.* *(Exod 14:23)* *And the Egyptians pursued, and went in after them to the midst of the sea, even all Pharaoh's horses, his chariots, and his horsemen.* *(Exod 14:24)* *And it came to pass, that in the morning watch the LORD looked unto the host of the Egyptians through the pillar of fire and of the cloud, and troubled the host of the Egyptians,* *(Exod 14:25)* *And took off their chariot wheels, that they drave them heavily: so that the Egyptians said, Let us flee from the face of Israel; for the LORD fighteth for them against the Egyptians.* *(Exod 14:26)* *And the LORD said unto Moses, Stretch out thine hand over the sea, that the waters may come again upon the Egyptians, upon their chariots, and upon their horsemen.* *(Exod 14:27)* *And Moses stretched forth his hand over the sea, and the sea returned to his strength when the morning appeared; and the Egyptians fled against it; and the LORD overthrew the Egyptians in the midst of the sea.* *(Exod 14:28)* *And the waters returned, and covered the chariots, and the horsemen, and all the host of Pharaoh that came into the sea after them; there remained not so much as one of them.* *(Exod 14:29)* *But the children of Israel* <u>**walked upon dry land in the midst of the sea**</u>*;*

and the waters were a wall unto them on their right hand, and on their left.

The Faith to Go over Obstacles

Heb 11:30 <u>**By faith**</u> the walls of Jericho fell down, after they were compassed about seven days.

> *Note: C.R. (**Josh 6:1**) Now Jericho was straitly shut up because of the children of Israel: none went out, and none came in. (**Josh 6:2**) And the LORD said unto Joshua, See, I have given into thine hand Jericho, and the king thereof, and the mighty men of valour. (**Josh 6:3**) And <u>ye shall compass the city, all ye men of war, and go round about the city once. Thus shalt thou do six days</u>. (**Josh 6:4**) And seven priests shall bear before the ark seven trumpets of rams' horns: and <u>the seventh day ye shall compass the city seven times</u>, and the priests shall blow with the trumpets. (**Josh 6:5**) And it shall come to pass, that <u>**when they make a long blast with the ram's horn, and when ye hear the sound of the trumpet, all the people shall shout with a great shout; and the wall of the city shall fall down flat**</u>, and the people shall ascend up every man straight before him.*

The Faith of Rahab

Heb 11:31 <u>**By faith**</u> the harlot Rahab perished not with **them that believed not**, when she had received the spies with peace.

> *Note: Their destruction was because of their unbelief.*

*Note: C.R. (**Josh 6:17**) And the city shall be accursed, even it, and all that are therein, to the LORD: only Rahab the harlot shall live, she and all that are with her in the house, because she hid the messengers that we sent.*

The Faith of Others

Heb 11:32 And what shall I more say? for the time would fail me to tell of **Gedeon**, and [of] **Barak**, and [of] **Samson**, and [of] **Jephthae**; [of] **David** also, and **Samuel**, and [of] **the prophets**:

Note: C.R. Gedeon (Judges 6-8) Barak (Judges 4-5) Samson (Judges 13-16) Jephthae (Judges 11-12) David (I Sam. 16-I Kings 2; I Chron. 11-29) Samuel (I Sam. 1-28)

Heb 11:33 Who **through faith** subdued kingdoms, wrought righteousness, obtained promises, stopped the mouths of lions,

*Note: "stopped the mouths of lions" (**Dan 6:22**) My God hath sent his angel, and hath **shut the lions' mouths**, that they have not hurt me: forasmuch as before him innocency was found in me; and also before thee, O king, have I done no hurt.*

Heb 11:34 Quenched the violence of fire, escaped the edge of the sword, out of weakness were made strong, waxed valiant in fight, turned to flight the armies of the aliens.

*Note: "quenched the violence of fire" (**Dan 3:19**) Then was Nebuchadnezzar full of fury, and the form of his visage*

*was changed against Shadrach, Meshach, and Abednego: therefore he spake, and commanded that they should heat the furnace one seven times more than it was wont to be heated. (**Dan 3:20**) And he commanded the most mighty men that were in his army to bind Shadrach, Meshach, and Abednego, and to cast them into the burning fiery furnace. (**Dan 3:21**) Then these men were bound in their coats, their hosen, and their hats, and their other garments, and <u>were cast into the midst of the burning fiery furnace</u>. (**Dan 3:22**) Therefore because the king's commandment was urgent, and the furnace exceeding hot, the flame of the fire slew those men that took up Shadrach, Meshach, and Abednego. (**Dan 3:23**) And these three men, <u>Shadrach, Meshach, and Abednego, fell down bound into the midst of the burning fiery furnace</u>. (**Dan 3:24**) Then Nebuchadnezzar the king was astonied, and rose up in haste, and spake, and said unto his counsellors, Did not we cast three men bound into the midst of the fire? They answered and said unto the king, True, O king. (**Dan 3:25**) He answered and said, Lo, I see four men loose, walking in the midst of the fire, and they have no hurt; and the form of the fourth is like the Son of God.*

Faith through Torture

Heb 11:35 Women received their dead raised to life again: and **others were tortured**, not accepting deliverance; that they might obtain a better resurrection:

Note: "women received their dead raised to life again"

*(2Kgs 4:32) And when **Elisha** was come into the house, behold, **the child was dead**, and laid upon his bed. (2Kgs 4:33) He went in therefore, and shut the door upon them twain, and prayed unto the LORD. (2Kgs 4:34) And he went up, and lay upon the child, and put his mouth upon his mouth, and his eyes upon his eyes, and his hands upon his hands: and he stretched himself upon the child; and the flesh of the child waxed warm. (2Kgs 4:35) Then he returned, and walked in the house to and fro; and went up, and stretched himself upon him: and **the child sneezed seven times, and the child opened his eyes**. (2Kgs 4:36) And he called Gehazi, and said, Call this Shunammite. So he called her. And when she was come in unto him, he said, Take up thy son. (2Kgs 4:37) Then she went in, and fell at his feet, and bowed herself to the ground, and took up her son, and went out.*

*(1Kgs 17:21) And he stretched himself upon the child three times, and cried unto the LORD, and said, O LORD my God, I pray thee, **let this child's soul come into him again**. (1Kgs 17:22) And the LORD heard the voice of Elijah; and the **soul of the child came into him again, and he revived.** (1Kgs 17:23) And Elijah took the child, and brought him down out of the chamber into the house, and delivered him unto his mother: and **Elijah** said, See, thy son liveth. (1Kgs 17:24) And the woman said to **Elijah**, Now by this I know that thou art a man of God, and that the word of the LORD in thy mouth is truth.*

Note: "resurrection" [386][42x][resurrection-39; rising again; that should rise; raised to life again]

Note: "a better resurrection" Please understand, because of trusting Christ as your Savior you are guaranteed by God eternal life and Heaven when you die. However, God will reward and recognize and honor believers who served God faithfully and those believers who were tortured and martyred for the cause of Christ with crowns, rewards, and reigning positions in heaven.

Faith Trough Torture

Heb 11:36 And others had trial of [cruel] mockings and scourgings, yea, moreover of bonds and imprisonment:

Heb 11:37 They were stoned, they were sawn asunder, were tempted, were slain with the sword: they wandered about in sheepskins and goatskins; being destitute, afflicted, tormented;

Note: Knowing of the torture that the saints of old have gone through and of the torture of some saints today, this should give us boldness toward God and help us see how good we have it and how God is.

Faith through Suffering

Heb 11:38 (Of whom the world was not worthy:) they wandered in deserts, and [in] mountains, and [in] dens and caves of the earth.

Faith Brings a Good Report

Heb 11:39 And these all, having obtained a good report **through faith**, received not the promise:

Heb 11:40 God having provided some better thing for us, that they without us should not be made perfect.

Note: Surely seeing the price that has been paid in the past for the faith, it will encourage us not to take the faith from the Bible for granted and pass it on to the next generation.

14

Hebrews Chapter 12

A Great Cloud of Witnesses
The Christian Life likened unto a Foot Race

Heb 12:1 Wherefore seeing we also are compassed about with so great a cloud of **witnesses**, let us lay aside every weight, and the sin which doth so easily beset [us], and let us run with patience the **race** that is set before us,

Note: "run with patience" It is important to note that there are two kinds of runners on any given track team. There is the sprinter and there is the long-distance runner. The scriptures here at verse 1 are referring to the long-distance runner as the one that is to run with patience. The end of your race as a long-distance runner is when you die.

Note: "compassed about" [#4029][5x][hanged about-2; am bound with; compassed about-2]

Note: "witnesses" [#3144][34x](witness-29; record-2; martyr–3)

See the following passages on martyrs.

Acts 22:20 *And when the blood of thy* **martyr** *Stephen was shed, I also was standing by, and consenting unto his death, and kept the raiment of them that slew him.*

Rev 2:13 *I know thy works, and where thou dwellest, even where Satan's seat is: and thou holdest fast my name, and hast not denied my faith, even in those days wherein Antipas was my faithful* **martyr***, who was slain among you, where Satan dwelleth.*

Rev 17:6 *And I saw the woman drunken with the blood of the saints, and with the blood of the* **martyrs** *of Jesus: and when I saw her, I wondered with great admiration.*

Note: "race" [#73][6x][race; conflict-2; contention; **fight***-2]*

2Tim 4:7 *I have fought a good* **fight***, I have finished my course, I have kept the faith:*

Note: The Christian life is not only compared to a foot race, but also a fight and a conflict.

Note: Some things that are not sin in themselves but if we let them hinder our service for God, they can become a weight and a sin.

2Tim 2:4 *No man that warreth entangleth himself with the affairs of this life; that he may please him who hath chosen him to be a soldier.*

Note: Seeing we have such a mighty army that has gone before us, and what great witnesses they were, we are challenged being on the same team to continue the relay race and to run well for the cause of Christ.

Note: "which doth so easily beset" [#2139][1x][def. skillfully surrounding or besetting: def. beset: to attack from all sides; to harass]

Note: The witnesses are witnesses that have given out the gospel in their life time and have died and many were mentioned in chapter 11, not witnesses that have died and are watching what is taking place down here on earth now.

Note: This passage is not teaching us that people in heaven can see us now down here on Earth. Why would someone enjoying the splendors of heaven want to look down here on this world of sinful activities?

The Example of Christ

Heb 12:2 Looking unto **Jesus the author and finisher of [our] faith**; who for the joy that was set before him endured the cross, despising the shame, and is set down at the right hand of the throne of God.

Note: "author" [#747][4x][Prince-2; captain; author]

Note: "finisher" [#5051][1x][rt. # 5048 - perfected; fulfilled]

Note: Jesus is the author (captain; prince) and finisher (perfecter) of our faith.

Heb 12:3 For consider him that endured such contradiction of sinners against himself, lest ye be **<u>wearied</u>** and faint in your minds.

Note: "wearied" [#2577][3x][sick; fainted; wearied]

Note: If we will think about what Jesus went through for us, that alone will get us through whatever trouble we are in and help us not to quit or give up. Ye have not yet resisted unto blood, striving against sin.

Note: Our battle is against sin, to keep ourselves pure but for the sinner to get the gospel to them and to edify the believer.

Eph 6:12 For we wrestle not against flesh and blood, but against principalities, against powers, against the rulers of the darkness of this world, against spiritual wickedness in high places.

Heb 12:4 Ye have not yet resisted unto blood, striving against sin.

The Chastening Hand of God
(One of the Marks of a True Believer)

Heb 12:5 And ye have forgotten the **exhortation** which speaketh unto you as unto children, My son, despise not thou the **chastening** of the Lord, nor faint when thou art **rebuked** of him:

Note: "exhortation" [#3874][29x][consolation-14; exhortation-8; comfort-6; intreaty]

Note: "chastening" [#3809][6x][chastening-3; chastisement; nurture; instruction]

Note: "rebuked" [#1651][17x][tell fault; convicted; reproved-6; rebuke-5; convinced-4]

Heb 12:6 For whom the Lord loveth he **chasteneth**, and scourgeth **every son** whom he receiveth.

Note: "chasteneth" [#3811][13x][chasten-6; chastise-2; learned-2; taught; instructing; teaching]

Note: There will be progressive change or chastisement from God present in every child of God. One of the marks of a true believer is God's chastening hand in their lives when they get into sin.

Heb 12:7 If ye endure chastening, God dealeth with you as with sons; for what son is he whom the father **chasteneth** not?

Note: "chastening" [#3809][6x][chastening-3; chastisement; nurture; instruction]

Note: This is why, even though saved and promised heaven, the child of God cannot do anything he wants to do that is wrong. God will chastise him for his own good.

Heb 12:8 But if ye be without **chastisement**, whereof all are partakers, then are ye bastards, and not sons.

Note: "chastening" [#3809][6x][chastening-3; chastisement; nurture; instruction][rt. # 3811]

Note: If you do not experience some form of chastisement from God for your sin in your life, you are not saved. So, if you can go out and do anything wrong you want to do without chastisement, you are lost. When God uses this term that means illegitimate it means that God is not their heavenly Father.

Heb 12:9 Furthermore we have had fathers of our flesh which **corrected** [us], and we gave [them] reverence: shall we not much rather be in subjection unto the Father of spirits, and live?

Note: "corrected" [#3810][2x][corrected; instructor][rt. # 3811]

Heb 12:10 For they verily for a few days **chastened** [us] after their own pleasure; but he for [our] profit, that [we] might be partakers of his holiness.

Note: "chasteneth" [#3811][13x][chasten-6; chastise-2; instruct; learn-2; teach-2]

Note: God's chastening hand is to make us better and for our own good.

The Fruit of God's Chastening Hand

Heb 12:11 Now no **chastening** for the present seemeth to be joyous, but grievous: nevertheless afterward it yieldeth the peaceable fruit of righteousness unto them which are **exercised** thereby.

Note: "exercised" [1128][4x][exercise-4] See the following passages of scripture.

Good Exercise

1Tim 4:7 *But refuse profane and old wives' fables, and **exercise** thyself rather unto*

Good Exercise

Heb 5:14 *But strong meat belongeth to them that are of full age, even those who by reason of use have their senses **exercised** to discern both good and evil.*

Bad Exercise

2Pet 2:14 *Having eyes full of adultery, and that cannot cease from sin; beguiling unstable souls: an heart they have **exercised** with covetous practices; cursed children:*

Other Passages on God's Chastisement

(Deut 8:5) *Thou shalt also consider in thine heart, that,* **as a man chasteneth his son, so the LORD thy God chasteneth thee.**

(2Sam 7:14) **I will be his father, and he shall be my son. If he commit iniquity, I will chasten him with the rod of men, and with the stripes of the children**

of men: (2Sam 7:15) <u>**But my mercy shall not depart**</u> <u>**away from him**</u>, *as I took it from Saul, whom I put away before thee.*

(Job 5:17) *Behold,* <u>**happy is the man whom God**</u> <u>**correcteth: therefore despise not thou the chastening**</u> <u>**of the Almighty**</u>:

(Ps 89:31) <u>**If they break my statutes, and keep not**</u> <u>**my commandments**</u>; *(Ps 89:32)* <u>**Then will I visit their**</u> <u>**transgression with the rod, and their iniquity with**</u> <u>**stripes.**</u> *(Ps 89:33)* <u>**Nevertheless my lovingkindness**</u> <u>**will I not utterly take from him, nor suffer my**</u> <u>**faithfulness to fail.**</u> *(Ps 89:34)* <u>**My covenant will I not**</u> <u>**break, nor alter the thing that is gone out of my lips.**</u>

(Ps 94:12) <u>**Blessed is the man whom thou chastenest,**</u> <u>**O LORD, and teachest him out of thy law;**</u>

(Prov 3:11) <u>**My son, despise not the chastening of the**</u> <u>**LORD; neither be weary of his correction:**</u>

(1Cor 11:32) *But* <u>**when we are judged, we are chastened**</u> <u>**of the Lord, that we should not be condemned with**</u> <u>**the world.**</u>

(Rev 3:19) <u>**As many as I love, I rebuke and chasten:**</u> <u>**be zealous therefore, and repent.**</u>

Diligence to Live Right

Heb 12:12 Wherefore lift up the hands which hang down, and the feeble knees;

Heb 12:13 And make straight paths for your feet, lest that which is lame be **turned out of the way**; but let it rather be healed.

Note: "straight" [#3717][2x][straight; upright]

Note: "turned out of the way" [#1624][5x][turn aside-2; avoid; turn; turn out of the way]

Note: The "lame" in v.13 is the "feeble knees" in v. 12. Unless we go with God's help we will be turned aside and side tracked getting off on the wrong path.

Follow Peace by Following God

Heb 12:14 Follow peace with all [men], and holiness, without which no man shall see the Lord:

Note: We follow God's peace not ours and God's holiness not ours.

Note: "holiness" [#38][10x][holiness-5; sanctification-5]

Note: This passage is not referring to man's own holiness that he would try to produce from his own works, but of God's holiness which is imputed unto him from salvation. Remember all our righteousness are as filthy rags.

*(Isa 64:6) But we are all as an unclean thing, and **all our righteousnesses are as filthy rags**; and we all do fade as a leaf; and our iniquities, like the wind, have taken us away.*

*Matt 5:20 For I say unto you, That **except your righteousness shall exceed the righteousness of the scribes and Pharisees, ye shall in no case enter into the kingdom of heaven.***

*Rom 3:22 Even **the righteousness of God which is by faith of Jesus Christ unto all and upon all them that believe**: for there is no difference:*

II Thess. 2:13 God hath from the beginning chosen you to salvation through sanctification of the Spirit and belief of the truth.

***Sanctification** here is translated from the same Greek word as the one that is translated into **holiness**.*

*I Cor. 1:30 But of him are ye in Christ Jesus, who of God is made unto us wisdom, and righteousness, and **sanctification**, and redemption:*

Keep Your Eyes on Jesus

Heb 12:15 Looking diligently lest any man <u>fail of the grace of God</u>; lest any root of bitterness springing up trouble [you], and thereby many be defiled;

*Note: "looking diligently" to Jesus, See v.2; also "the grace of God" mentioned here is more than (**saving grace**). It is (**serving grace**). Notice the following passages.*

Saving Grace

Eph 2:8 <u>**For by grace are ye saved through faith**</u>; *and that not of yourselves: it is the gift of God:* **9** *Not of works, lest any man should boast.*

Serving Grace

Heb. 12:28 *Wherefore we receiving a kingdom which cannot be moved,* <u>**let us have grace, whereby we may serve God acceptably**</u> *with reverence and godly fear:*

*If we as God's people do not keep our eyes on Jesus, we will come short of the grace from God that we need to serve God acceptably with reverence and godly fear and come short of the (**suffering grace**) we will need in times of trials and trouble. See the following passage.*

Suffering Grace

2Cor 12:9 *And he said unto me,* <u>**My grace**</u> *is sufficient for thee: for my strength is made perfect in weakness.* <u>**Most gladly therefore will I rather glory in my infirmities, that the power of Christ may rest upon me**</u>.

*Just like we need God's (**saving grace**) to get us to heaven, we need God's (**serving grace**) in order to serve God acceptably and God's (**suffering grace**) to get us* *through trials. Otherwise, any attempt to go or do without (God's grace) will result in bitterness and in poor judgment concerning the things of God and hurt the cause of Christ.*

Note: Before we continue on in the verse by verse study, this author deems it necessary to go over the three doorways to God's amazing grace.

Three doorways to grace:

1. ***Faith****: The contrast is doubt or relying on other things besides God.*

    Romans 4:16 *Therefore* ***it is of faith, that it might be by grace****; to the end the promise might be sure to all the seed; not to that only which is of the law, but to that also which is of the faith of Abraham; who is the father of us all,*

    Romans 5:2 *By whom also we have* ***access by faith into this grace*** *wherein we stand, and rejoice in hope of the glory of God.*

2. ***Humility****: The contrast is pride and self-sufficiency*

    James 4:6 *But he giveth more grace. Wherefore he saith, God resisteth the proud, but* ***giveth grace unto the humble.***

    1 Peter 5:5 *Likewise, ye younger, submit yourselves unto the elder. Yea, all of you be subject one to another, and be clothed with humility: for God resisteth the proud, and* ***giveth grace to the humble****.*

3. ***Prayer***: *The contrast is refusal to ask for help*
   Hebrews 4:16 *Let us therefore come boldly unto the throne of grace, that we may obtain mercy, and find grace to help in time of need.*

The Example of Esau

Heb 12:16 Lest there [be] any fornicator, or **profane person, as Esau**, who for one morsel of meat sold his birthright.

Note: C.R. ***Gen 25:29*** *And Jacob sod pottage: and Esau came from the field, and he was faint:* ***30*** *And Esau said to Jacob, Feed me, I pray thee, with that same red pottage; for I am faint: therefore was his name called Edom.* ***31*** *And Jacob said, Sell me this day thy birthright.* ***32*** *And Esau said, Behold, I am at the point to die: and what profit shall this birthright do to me?* ***33*** *And Jacob said, Swear to me this day; and he sware unto him: and he sold his birthright unto Jacob.* ***34*** *Then Jacob gave Esau bread and pottage of lentiles; and he did eat and drink, and rose up, and went his way: thus Esau despised his birthright.*

Heb 12:17 For ye know how that afterward, when he would have inherited the blessing, **he was rejected: for he found no place of repentance**, though he sought it carefully with tears.

Note: Esau found no place of repentance in his dad, Isaac. It was Esau that was trying to get his dad, Isaac, to change his mind or repent and it was the dad, Isaac, that would not change his mind or repent.

Note: C.R. **Gen 27:30** *And it came to pass, as soon as Isaac had made an end of blessing Jacob, and Jacob was yet scarce gone out from the presence of Isaac his father, that Esau his brother came in from his hunting.* **31** *And he also had made savoury meat, and brought it unto his father, and said unto his father, Let my father arise, and eat of his son's venison, that thy soul may bless me.* **32** *And Isaac his father said unto him, Who art thou? And he said, I am thy son, thy firstborn Esau.* **33** *And Isaac trembled very exceedingly, and said, Who? where is he that hath taken venison, and brought it me, and **I have eaten of all before thou camest, and have blessed him? yea, and he shall be blessed**.* **34** *And when Esau heard the words of his father, he cried with a great and exceeding bitter cry, and said unto his father, Bless me, even me also, O my father.* **35** *And he said, Thy brother came with subtilty, and hath taken away thy blessing.* **36** *And he said, Is not he rightly named Jacob? for he hath supplanted me these two times: he took away my birthright; and, behold, now he hath taken away my blessing. And **he said, Hast thou not reserved a blessing for me?*** **37** *And Isaac answered and said unto Esau, Behold, **I have made him thy lord, and all his brethren have I given to him for servants; and with corn and wine have I sustained him**: and what shall I do now unto thee, my son?* **38** *And Esau said unto his father, Hast thou but one blessing, my father? bless me, even me also, O my father. And Esau lifted up his voice, and wept.* **39** ***And Isaac his father answered and said unto him, Behold, thy dwelling shall be the fatness of the earth, and of the dew of heaven from above***; **40** ***And by thy sword shalt thou live, and shalt***

serve thy brother; and it shall come to pass when thou shalt have the dominion, that thou shalt break his yoke from off thy neck.

Note: Esau was seeking repentance from his father, Isaac, not repentance within himself. In other words, Esau was hoping Isaac would change his mind about his decision of Jacob receiving the blessing and give the blessing to Esau instead. So, it was Esau's dad who would not change his mind and not Esau.

The Meeting at the Mount

Heb 12:18 For ye are not come unto the mount that might be touched, and that burned with fire, nor unto blackness, and darkness, and tempest,

Heb 12:19 And the sound of a trumpet, and the voice of words; which [voice] they that heard intreated that the word should not be spoken to them any more:

Heb 12:20 (For they could not endure that which was commanded, And if so much as a beast touch the mountain, it shall be stoned, or thrust through with a dart:

Heb 12:21 And so terrible was the sight, [that] Moses said, I exceedingly fear and quake:)

Note: "terrible" [5398][3 times][fearful; terrible-2]

Note: C.R. for v. 18-21 Notice the following passage of scripture.

*(Exod 19:12) And thou shalt set bounds unto the people round about, saying, Take heed to yourselves, **that ye go not up into the mount, or touch the border of it: whosoever toucheth the mount shall be surely put to death**: (Exod 19:13) **There shall not an hand touch it, but he shall surely be stoned, or shot through**; **whether it be beast or man, it shall not live**: **when the trumpet soundeth long**, they shall come up to the mount. (Exod 19:14) And Moses went down from the mount unto the people, and sanctified the people; and they washed their clothes. (Exod 19:15) And he said unto the people, Be ready against the third day: come not at your wives. (Exod 19:16) And it came to pass on the third day in the morning, that there **were thunders and lightnings, and a thick cloud upon the mount, and the voice of the trumpet exceeding loud**; so that all the people that was in the camp trembled. (Exod 19:17) And Moses brought forth the people out of the camp to meet with God; and they stood at the nether part of the mount. (Exod 19:18) And mount Sinai was altogether on a smoke, because the LORD descended upon it in fire: and the smoke thereof ascended as the smoke of a furnace, and the whole mount quaked greatly. (Exod 19:19) And when **the voice of the trumpet sounded long, and waxed louder and louder**, Moses spake, and God answered him by a voice. (Exod 19:20) And the LORD came down upon mount Sinai, on the top of the mount: and the LORD called Moses up to the top of the mount; and Moses went up. (Exod 19:21) And the LORD said unto Moses, Go down, charge the people, lest they break through unto the LORD to gaze, and many of them perish. (Exod 19:22) And let the priests*

*also, which come near to the LORD, sanctify themselves, lest the LORD break forth upon them. (**Exod 19:23**) And Moses said unto the LORD, The people cannot come up to mount Sinai: for thou chargedst us, saying, Set bounds about the mount, and sanctify it. (**Exod 19:24**) And the LORD said unto him, Away, get thee down, and thou shalt come up, thou, and Aaron with thee: but let not the priests and the people break through to come up unto the LORD, lest he break forth upon them. (**Exod 20:18**) And all the people **<u>saw the thunderings, and the lightnings, and the noise of the trumpet</u>**, and the mountain smoking: and when the people saw it, they removed, and stood afar off. (**Exod 20:19**) And they said unto Moses, Speak thou with us, and we will hear: but let not God speak with us, lest we die. (**Exod 20:20**) And Moses said unto the people, Fear not: for God is come to prove you, and that his fear may be before your faces, that ye sin not. (**Exod 20:21**) And the people stood afar off, and Moses drew near unto the thick darkness where God was.*

Note: Better than what Moses saw on earth is what we will see in heaven.

The Meeting at Mount Sion

Heb 12:22 But ye are come unto mount Sion, and unto the city of the living God, the heavenly Jerusalem, and to an innumerable company of angels,

Heb 12:23 To the general assembly and church of the firstborn, **<u>which are written in heaven</u>**, and to God the Judge of all, and to the spirits of just men made perfect,

Note: "written in heaven" Notice the following passages.

*(**Phil 4:3**) And I intreat thee also, true yokefellow, help those women which laboured with me in the gospel, with Clement also, and with other my fellowlabourers, **whose names are in the book of life.***

*(**Luke 10:20**) Notwithstanding in this rejoice not, that the spirits are subject unto you; but rather rejoice, because **your names are written in heaven**.*

*(**Rev 13:8**) And all that dwell upon the earth shall worship him, **whose names are not written in the book of life of the Lamb** slain from the foundation of the world.*

*(**Rev 17:8**) The beast that thou sawest was, and is not; and shall ascend out of the bottomless pit, and go into perdition: and they that dwell on the earth shall wonder, **whose names were not written in the book of life** from the foundation of the world, when they behold the beast that was, and is not, and yet is.*

Note: "the spirits of just men made perfect" This tells us there is no such thing as 'soul sleep'. These spirits of just men are waiting in heaven.

Note: We see in heaven, not only the city, angels, the church, God the Father, the souls of saved people, and Jesus but also the blood of Christ placed in the temple like the priests placed in the tabernacle on earth. [See v. 24]

Heb 12:24 And to **<u>Jesus the mediator</u>** of the new covenant, and to the blood of sprinkling, that speaketh better things than [that of] Abel.

Note: "mediator" [3316][6 times][All translated "mediator"]

Jesus is the only Mediator

*(1Tim 2:5) For there is one God, and **<u>one mediator between God and men, the man Christ Jesus;</u>***

*(Heb 8:6) But now hath he obtained a more excellent ministry, by how much also **<u>he is the mediator</u>** of a better covenant, which was established upon better promises.*

*(Heb 9:15) And for this cause **<u>he is the mediator</u>** of the new testament, that by means of death, for the redemption of the transgressions that were under the first testament, they which are called might receive the promise of eternal inheritance.*

Note: Abel's blood cried out to God for vengeance for himself but Jesus' blood cries out to God for mercy.

(Gen 4:10) And he said, What hast thou done? the voice of thy brother's blood crieth unto me from the ground.

The Price of Refusing

Heb 12:25 See that ye refuse not him that speaketh. For if they escaped not who refused him that spake on earth, much more [shall not] we [escape], if we turn away from him that [speaketh] from heaven:

Note: "refuse" [3868][11 times][avoid; make excuse; excuse-2; intreat; refuse-5; reject]

Note: There is no way the believer can escape the chastening hand of God if they refuse to listen to the Holy Spirit or God's word. Making excuses or avoiding is the same as rejecting him. Also, there is no way the unbeliever can escape Hell if they refuse to trust Christ as their Savior.

The Temporary versus the Eternal

Heb 12:26 Whose voice then shook the earth: but now he hath promised, saying, Yet once more I shake not the earth only, but also heaven.

Note: C.R. See the following passages.

*(Isa 13:13) Therefore **I will shake the heavens, and the earth shall remove out of her place**, in the wrath of the LORD of hosts, and in the day of his fierce anger.*

*(Joel 3:16) The LORD also shall roar out of Zion, and utter his voice from Jerusalem; and **the heavens and the earth shall shake**: but the LORD will be the hope of his people, and the strength of the children of Israel.*

*(Hag 2:6) For thus saith the LORD of hosts; **Yet once**, it is a little while, and **I will shake the heavens, and the earth, and the sea, and the dry land**;*

Heb 12:27 And this [word], Yet once more, signifieth the removing of those things that are shaken, as of things that are made, that those things which cannot be shaken may remain.

Note: "removing" [3331][3 times][change-Heb. 7:12; translation-Heb.11:5]

Note: (a few of the things that cannot be shaken) Jesus; the bible; our salvation; God and his promises:

Serving Grace

Heb 12:28 Wherefore we receiving a kingdom which cannot be moved, let us have grace, whereby we may serve God acceptably with reverence and godly fear:

Note: "serve" [3000][21x][4-worship; 17-serve]

Note: "acceptably" [2102][1x][rt.# 2101][9 times][acceptable-5] [wellpleasing-4]

Note: Just like we cannot get saved without God's grace, we cannot serve God without God's grace. We can actually serve God and still not be pleasing to him, if we do it without God's grace with reverence and godly fear.

Our God is:

Heb 12:29 For <u>**our God [is] a consuming fire**</u>.

Note: God is able (Matt. 3:9)(Luke 3:8)(Rom. 11:23) (Rom. 14:4)(II Cor. 9:8)

> *God is not the God of the dead, but of the living (Matt. 22:32)*
> *God is one Lord (Mark 12:29)*
> *God is true (John 3:33)(II Cor. 1:18)*
> *God is a Spirit (John 4:24)*
> *God is no respecter of persons (Acts 10:34)*
> *God is faithful (I Cor. 1:9)(I Cor. 10:13)*
> *God is not the author of confusion (I Cor. 14:33)*
> *God is one (Gal. 3:20)*
> *God is not mocked (Gal. 6:7)*
> *God is witness (I Thess. 2:5)*
> *God is not unrighteous (Heb. 6:10)*
> *God is a consuming fire (Hev. 12:29)*
> *God is light (I John 1:5)*
> *God is love (I John 4:8)(I John 4:16)*

15

Hebrews Chapter 13

Love the Brotherhood

Heb 13:1 Let brotherly love continue.

Note: "brotherly love" [5360] Philadelphia [6x][brotherly love-3; brotherly kindness-2; love of the brethren]

Love the Strangers

Heb 13:2 Be not forgetful to **entertain strangers**: for thereby some have **entertained** angels unawares.

*Note: "entertain strangers" [5381][2x][entertain strangers; given to hospitality-**Rom.12:13**]*

Note: "entertained" [#3579][10x][entertained; lodge-6; think it strange-2; strange]

Care for Those Having Hard Times

Heb 13:3 Remember them that are in **bonds**, as bound with them; [and] them which **suffer adversity**, as being yourselves also in the body.

> *Note: "bonds" [1198][16x][prisoner-14; be in bonds; in bonds]*

> *Note: "suffer adversity" [2558][2x][suffer adversity; tormented-**Heb. 11:37**]*

> *Note: Put yourselves in the place of the suffering individual that you might have the proper compassion and burden to care and pray for them.*

True Marriage versus Living Together Outside of Marriage

Heb 13:4 Marriage [is] **honourable** in all, and the **bed** undefiled: but **whoremongers** and adulterers God will judge.

> *Note: "marriage" [#1062][16x][wedding-7; marriage-9]*

> *Note: "honourable" [5093][14x][honourable; in reputation; dear; precious-11]*

> *Note: "bed" [#2845][4x][conceived; bed-2; chambering-**Rom. 13:13**]*

> *Note: "whoremongers" [#4205][10 times][whoremonger-5; fornicators-5]*

Note: Marriage is more than just a piece of paper as some suppose. It is honorable, dear, and precious in the eyes of God and it is the difference between the blessing of God and the judgment of God on those who live together outside of marriage.

"chambering". **Rom 13:13** *Let us walk honestly, as in the day; not in rioting and drunkenness, not in __chambering__ and wantonness, not in strife and envying.*

Contentment with Christ

Heb 13:5 [Let your] conversation [be] without covetousness; [and be] content with such things as ye have: for he hath said, I will never leave thee, nor forsake thee.

Note: "content" [#714][8x][be content-3; enough; sufficient-2; sufficeth; content]

Note: We need not be greedy or covetousness. We can live in contentment when we remember that Jesus will never leave us by ourselves.

The Lord is our Ever-present Helper

Heb 13:6 So that we may boldly say, __The Lord [is] my helper, and I will not fear what man shall do unto me.__

Note: See the following passages.

2Tim 1:7 *For God hath not given us the spirit of fear; but of power, and of love, and of a sound mind.*

Matt 10:28 *And fear not them which kill the body, but are not able to kill the soul: but rather fear him which is able to destroy both soul and body in hell.*

Luke 12:4 *And I say unto you my friends, Be not afraid of them that kill the body, and after that have no more that they can do.5 But I will forewarn you whom ye shall fear: Fear him, which after he hath killed hath power to cast into hell; yea, I say unto you, Fear him.*

(Ps 46:1) <u>**God is our refuge and strength, a very present help in trouble**</u>.

Those in Authority

Heb 13:7 Remember them which have the rule over you, who have spoken unto you the word of God: whose faith follow, considering the end of [their] conversation.

Note: Although the bible teaches elsewhere to honor and pray for our government and leaders, this is not talking of our secular leaders. This is talking of our pastor and spiritual leaders at church.

Jesus is Perfect and Can Not Change

Heb 13:8 Jesus Christ the same yesterday, and to day, and for ever.

Note: When you are perfect you can't change because any change would make you less than perfect. Now this passage does not mean that God has never changed how he deals with man.

Notice the following examples]

> *The dietary laws have changed at least 3 times:*
> **[Gen. 1:29-30; Lev. 11; I Tim. 4:3-5]**

> *The law of circumcision has changed.*
> **[Gen. 17:10-27; Gal. 5:6; I Cor. 7:19]**

> *The sacrificial laws have been fulfilled.*
> **[Heb. 10:5-12]**

> *The sabbath days have been fulfilled.*
> **[Col. 2:14-17]**

> *Salvation and Jesus never will change.*

Warning of False Teachings

Heb 13:9 Be not carried about with divers and strange doctrines. For [it is] a good thing that the heart be established with grace; not with meats, which have not profited them that have been occupied therein.

Note: "divers" [#4164][10x][divers-8; manifold-2]

*Note: "doctrines" [#1322][30x][doctrine-29; hath been taught-**Tit. 1:9**]*

Note: "established" [#950][8x][confirmed-5; established-2; stablish]

Note: If a teaching you hear cannot be backed up by the Bible, disregard the teaching.

That which is Without the Camp and Without the Gate
Heb 13:10 We have an altar, whereof they have no right to eat which serve the tabernacle.

Heb 13:11 For the bodies of those beasts, whose blood is brought into the sanctuary by the high priest for sin, are burned **without the camp**.

Heb 13:12 Wherefore Jesus also, that he might sanctify the people with his own blood, suffered **without the gate**.

*Note: [the Blood Atonement][See **Heb. 9:12** for other verses.]*

Heb 13:13 Let us go forth therefore unto him **without the camp**, bearing his reproach.

Heavenly Minded

Heb 13:14 For here have we no continuing city, but **we seek one to come**.

The True Sacrifices for God

Heb 13:15 By him therefore let us offer the **sacrifice of praise to God continually, that is, the fruit of [our] lips giving thanks to his name**.

Note: These are the sacrifices God is wanting from us as God's people.

Rom. 12:1 *"present your bodies a living sacrifice"*

Psa. 107:22 *"sacrifice the sacrifices of thanksgiving"*
Psa. 116:17

Psa. 27:6 *"therefore will I offer in his tabernacle sacrifices of joy; I will sing, yea, I will sing praises unto the Lord."*

Psa. 51:17 *"The sacrifices of God are a broken spirit: a broken and a contrite heart, O God, thou wilt not despise."*

Heb 13:16 But **to do good and to communicate forget not**: for with such sacrifices God is well pleased.

Note: "communicate" [#2842][20x][fellowship-12; contribution; communion-4; to communicate; communication; distribution]

Those in Authority

Heb 13:17 Obey them that have the rule over you, and submit yourselves: for they watch for your souls, as they that must give account, that they may do it with joy, and not with grief: for that [is] unprofitable for you.

Note: "Obey" [3982][55x][persuaded-22; trusted-8; obey-7; agreed; friend; believed-3; yield; shall assure; confidence-6; be confident; misc-4]

*Note: Although the bible teaches elsewhere to honor and pray for our government leaders, this is not talking of our secular leadership. This is talking of our pastor and spiritual leaders in church. (See notes at **Heb. 13:7**)*

The Request for Prayer

Heb 13:18 Pray for us: for we trust we have a good conscience, in all things willing to live honestly.

Heb 13:19 But I beseech [you] the rather to do this, that I may be restored to you the sooner.

The God of Peace

Heb 13:20 Now the God of peace, that brought again from the dead <u>**our Lord Jesus, that great shepherd of the sheep**</u>, through the blood of the everlasting covenant,

Note: "shepherd" [#4166][18x][pastors-Eph. 4:11; 17 times-shepherd]

See the following passages.

*1Pet 2:25 For ye were as sheep going astray; but are now returned unto the <u>**Shepherd and Bishop of your souls**</u>.*

*John 10:2 But he that entereth in by the door is the <u>**shepherd of the sheep**</u>.*

*John 10:11 <u>**I am the good shepherd**</u>: the <u>**good shepherd giveth his life for the sheep**</u>. 12 But he that is an hireling,* *and not the shepherd, whose own the sheep are not, seeth the wolf coming, and leaveth the sheep, and fleeth: and the wolf catcheth them, and scattereth the sheep.*

John 10:14 <u>**I am the good shepherd**</u>, *and know my sheep, and am known of mine.*

John 10:16 *And other sheep I have, which are not of this fold: them also I must bring, and they shall hear my voice; and there shall be one fold, and* <u>**one shepherd**</u>.

Note: "the blood of the everlasting covenant" See notes at **Heb. 9:12**

The God of Perfection Working Perfection in Us

Heb 13:21 Make you perfect in every good work to do his will, working in you that which is well pleasing in his sight, through Jesus Christ; to whom [be] glory for ever and ever. Amen.

Note: C.R. **Phil 1:6** *Being confident of this very thing, that he which hath begun a good work in you will perform it until the day of Jesus Christ:*

Exhortation and a Personal Note and Signing Off

Heb 13:22 And I beseech you, brethren, **suffer** the word of **exhortation**: for I have written a letter unto you in **few words**.

Note: "suffer" [#430][15x][suffer-7; should bear with-4; forbearing-2; will endure-2]

Note: "exhortation" [#3874][29x][consolation-14; comfort-6; exhortation-8; intreaty]

Note: "few words" [#1024][7x][little while; little space; little-4; few words]

Heb 13:23 Know ye that [our] brother Timothy is **set at liberty**; with whom, if he come shortly, I will see you.

Note: "set at liberty" [#630][69x][release-17; put away-14; send away-13; dismissed; let go-13; set at liberty-2; let depart-2; dismiss-2; misc-5]

Note: Paul is waiting to receive escort from Timothy before he comes.

Heb 13:24 Salute all them that have the **rule over** you, and all the saints. They of Italy **salute** you.

Note: "salute" [#782][60x][salute-42; embraced-2; greet-15; take leave]

Note: "rule" [#2233][28x][count-10; think-4; esteem-3; be governor-2; have rule over-3; misc-6]

*See **Heb. 13:7, 17** concerning them that have the rule over you.]*

Heb 13:25 Grace [be] with you all. Amen.

16

A Concise Outline of the Book of James

Chapter 1:1	An Introduction to James
Chapter 1:2-4	The Right Perspective on Trials
Chapter 1:5	The Source of Wisdom
Chapter 1:6-9	Dealing with Holy Living
Chapter 1:10-11	Guidelines for the Rich
Chapter 1:12-16	Dealing with Temptation
Chapter 1:17	The Source of Good Things
Chapter 1:18	The New Birth Requires the Word of God
Chapter 1:19-21	Holy Living
Chapter 1:22-25	Dealing with the Word of God
Chapter 1:26-27	True Religion versus False Religion
Chapter 2:1-13	Dealing with Prejudice
Chapter 2:14-26	True Faith versus Vain Faith
Chapter 3:1	Responsibility
Chapter 3:2-13	Dealing with the Tongue

Chapter 3:14-16	**Dealing with Envy and Strife**
Chapter 3:17-18	**Heavenly Wisdom**
Chapter 4:1-5	**Dealing with Sinful Lusts**
Chapter 4:6-10	**Humility and Grace**
Chapter 4:11-12	**How we Should Deal with Others**
Chapter 4:13-16	**Dealing with the Future**
Chapter 4:17	**Sin Defined**
Chapter 5:1-6	**Dealing with the Rich**
Chapter 5:7-20	**Patience**

Before we get into a verse by verse study of the book of James, it is important to notice the many pairs that are mentioned in the book of James. See the following.

1) Two kinds of religion are mention in James 1:26-27. The true religion and the vain religion.

2) Two kinds of faith are mentioned in James 2:14-26. Genuine faith and dead faith.

3) Two kinds of justification are mentioned in James 2:21-26. Inward justification and outward justification.

4) Two kinds of wisdom are mentioned in James 3:15-17. Earthly wisdom and wisdom that is from above.

5) In James chapter 4 & 5 there is the proud versus the humble and the patient versus the impatient.

Enjoy searching out the other pairs mentioned in the book of James and now on to the verse by verse study.

17

James Chapter 1

An Introduction to James

James 1:1 James, a servant of God and of the Lord Jesus Christ, to the twelve tribes which are scattered abroad, greeting.

Note: This letter is addressed to the believing Jews but applies to all believers. This also tells us that at the time of this writing all twelve tribes of Israel existed.

The Right Perspective of Your Trials

James 1:2 My brethren, <u>count it all joy</u> when ye fall into divers temptations;

Note: "temptations" [#3986][21x][20-temptations ; 1-is to try]

*Note: [**I Pet. 1:7** "<u>the trial of your faith, being much more precious than gold</u>"]*

Note: What gives the trials and divers temptations a time of joy and so much value is that the time of trials is also a time of <u>learning</u> and a time of <u>improving</u> and a time of <u>growing while getting closer to God</u>. Notice the following.

Trials Produce Patience

James 1:3 Knowing [this], that the <u>trying of your faith worketh patience</u>.

Note: "trying" [1383][2x][trial-I Pet. 1:7]

Note: "worketh" [2716][24x][work-15; do-5; do deed; to perform; cause; work out]

Note: "patience" [5281][32x][3 times in James][patience-29; patient continuance; enduring; patient waiting]

Note: Since trials cause or produce patience, this is another reason why the trials are so valuable.

Romans 5:3-5 *And not only so, but we glory in tribulations also: knowing that <u>tribulation worketh patience</u>; 4 And patience, experience; and experience, hope: 5 And hope maketh not ashamed; because the love of God is shed abroad in our hearts by the Holy Ghost which is given unto us.*

Note the following statements from the Bible about patience.

Luke 8:15 *Bear fruit with patience.*
Luke 21:19 *In your patience possess ye your souls.*

I Thess. 5:14 *Be patient toward all men.*
I Tim. 3:3 *Patience is a requirement for pastors.*
Heb. 12:1 *Run with patience.*
Gal. 5:22 *Longsuffering, part of the fruit of the Spirit*

Note: The purpose and results of trials is also what makes them so valuable.

1 Peter 5:10 *But the God of all grace, who hath called us unto his eternal glory by Christ Jesus, <u>after that ye have suffered a while</u>, make you perfect, stablish, strengthen, settle you.*

1) *stablish you (#4741)(13x)(stablish-6; establish-3;strengthen-2; stedfastly set; fixed)*
2) *strengthen you*
3) *settle you (#2311)(6x)(founded-2; Matt. 7:25) (grounded-2; Col. 1:23; settle; lay foundation)*
4) *sanctify you -* **1 Peter 4:1** *Forasmuch then as Christ hath suffered for us in the flesh, arm yourselves likewise with the same mind: for* **<u>he that hath suffered in the flesh hath ceased from sin;</u>**

> **Luke 2:35** *(Yea, a sword shall pierce through thy own soul also,) that the thoughts of many hearts may be revealed.*
>
> *Note: Your trials will reveal:*
>
> 1) *who you really are*
> 2) *who your friends really are*

3) *who your enemies are*
4) *and most importantly, more about who God is*

Patience Produces Perfection

James 1:4 But let patience have [her] perfect work, that ye may be perfect and entire, wanting nothing.

Note: "perfect" [#5046][19x][perfect-17; men; of full age]

Note: "entire" [#3648][2x][whole-I Thess. 5:23]

Note: Don't panic when trials come. Learn as much as possible from your trials and let your trials push you closer to God. Notice the following passage.

*(**Rom 8:28**) And we know that all things work together for good to them that love God, to them who are the called according to his purpose.*

Let patience have her perfect work.

Source of Wisdom

James 1:5 If any of you lack wisdom, let him ask of God, that giveth to all [men] liberally, and upbraideth not; and it shall be given him.

Note: "wisdom" [#4678][51x](wisdom-51)[4 times in James]

Note: "upbraideth" [#3679](10x)(shall revile-2; cast in his teeth; reproached-3;suffer reproach; upbraid-3]

Note: We can ask for wisdom from God in general, but the direct application is to ask for wisdom during your trials in order to know what to do to be alert and to learn.

Dealing with Holy Living
Proper Praying

James 1:6 But let him ask in faith, nothing wavering. For he that wavereth is like a wave of the sea driven with the wind and tossed.

*Note: "wavering" [1252][19x][discern-2; **doubt-5**; put difference; staggered; contending-2; partial; judge-3; waver-2; misc-2]*

James 1:7 For let not that man think that he shall receive any thing of the Lord.

Note: There are many guidelines in the Bible on prayer that goes along with asking. (Please see this author's book on "Prayer.")

1) Ask without doubting:	*James 1:6-7*
2) Ask according to God's will	*I John 5:14*
3) Ask with a submissive heart	*I John 3:22*
4) Ask while giving proper respect to mate	*I Pet. 3:7*
5) Ask unselfishly	*James 4:2-3*

The Double Minded

James 1:8 A double minded man [is] unstable in all his ways.

Note: "double minded" [See James 4:8]

Note: "double minded" as in the divine nature versus the sinful nature and the believer yielding back and forth to each instead of starving the sinful nature and listening only to the divine nature.

Humility Brings Exaltation

James 1:9 Let the brother of **low degree** rejoice in that he is exalted:

Note: "low degree" [5011][8x](of low degree-2; low estate; lowly; base; humble-2; cast down]

__Note: Pride is very impatient__.

Guidelines for the Rich

James 1:10 But the rich, in that he is made low: because as the flower of the grass he shall pass away.

Note: "made low" [#5014][4x][low estate; humiliation; vile; made low]

Note: Some rich people have a tendency to be independent from God and full of pride.

Note: There are many commands and warnings in the New Testament concerning the rich:

*[See story of the rich young fool: **Luke 12:15-21**]*

1Tim 6:9 *But they that will be rich fall into temptation and a snare, and into many foolish and hurtful lusts, which drown men in destruction and perdition.* **10** *For the **love of money** is the root of all evil: which while some coveted after, they have erred from the faith, and pierced themselves through with many sorrows.*

1Tim 6:17 *Charge them that are rich in this world, that they **be not highminded**, **nor trust in uncertain riches**, **but in the living God**, who giveth us richly all things to enjoy;* **18** *That they **do good**, that they be **rich in good works**, **ready to distribute**, **willing to communicate**;* **19** *Laying up in store for themselves a good foundation against the time to come, that they may lay hold on eternal life.*

Notice the List of Commands Below Concerning the Rich

1) *Be not high-minded*
2) *Don't trust in uncertain riches.*
3) *Trust in the living God.*
4) *Do good.*
5) *Be rich in good works*
6) *Be ready to distribute.*
7) *Be willingly to communicate.*
8) *Make sure they are saved.*

James 1:11 For the sun is no sooner risen with a burning heat, but it withereth the grass, and the flower thereof falleth, and the grace of the fashion of it perisheth: so also shall the rich man fade away in his ways.

> *Note: "the rich man" [See **I Tim. 6:17** God has given us richly all things to enjoy.] It is not a sin to be rich. Example: Abraham, Isaac, Jacob, Job, and David were very wealthy men. The ways of some rich men are wicked because they are independent from God and full of pride. [**I Tim. 6:10** The love of money is the root of all evil.] It is not money that is the root of all evil. It is the love of money that is the root of all evil.*

Dealing with Temptation

James 1:12 Blessed [is] the man that <u>**endureth temptation**</u>: for when he is tried, he shall receive the crown of life, which the Lord hath promised to them that love him.

> *Note: "endureth" [#5278][17x](endure-11; tarry behind; abide; suffer; patient; take patiently-2)*

> *Note: "temptation" [#3986][21x][temptation-19; temptations; try]*

>> *To yield to temptation is to fail to endure temptation. To panic over the trials that come our way is to fail to endure temptation. To fail to learn from trials is to fail to endure temptation.*

> *Note: "tried" [#1384][7x](approved-6; tried)*

Note: The reward of "the crown of life" is given to the believer who loves God and endures temptation. It takes love for God to endure temptation.

Note: There are five crowns mentioned in the N.T. as rewards for the believer.

1) "**_crown of life_**" *James 1:12; Rev. 2:10* [for being faithful unto death, enduring temptation, and loving God.]

2) "**_incorruptible crown_**" *I Cor. 9:25* [for running well the Christian race.]

3) "**_crown of rejoicing_**" *I Thess. 2:19* [the soulwinner's crown]

4) "**_crown of righteousness_**" *II Tim. 4:8* [finishing God's purpose in your life] "fought a good fight-finished my course-kept the faith" and to those who will love Christ's appearing:

The person that quits on God and does not finish his purpose will not love Christ's appearing.

5) "**_crown of glory_**" *I Pet. 5:4* [the genuine pastor's crown]

Temptation to Sin Comes from Satan and The Sinful Nature And not from God

James 1:13 Let no man say when he is tempted, I am tempted of God: for God cannot be tempted with evil, neither tempteth he any man:

Note: "tempted" [#3985][39x)(tempt-29; try-4; tempter-2; prove; assayed; examine; go about)

Note: At no time will God try to get you to do wrong. Our God is holy and cannot be tempted to do wrong. Satan knows well that Jesus could not sin and could not be tempted to sin. However, it was the first time in all eternity that God was wrapped in human flesh, yet without sin.

James 1:14 But every man is tempted, when he is drawn away of his own lust, and enticed.

Note: "lust" [1939][38 times][desire-3; concupiscence-3; lust-31; lust after]

Note: "enticed" [#1185][3x)(enticed; beguiling; allure]

Note: It is Satan who appeals to our sinful nature, but a greater enemy than Satan is ourselves. Satan can hinder us, but it is we who decide to do wrong. Satan cannot make you do wrong, he can only make wrong look appealing.

Romans 7:18 *For I know that in me (that is, in my flesh,) dwelleth no good thing: for to will is present with me; but how to perform that which is good I find not.*

Sin's Goal Is to Kill

James 1:15 Then when lust hath conceived, it bringeth forth sin: and **sin, when it is finished, bringeth forth death.**

Note: "conceived" [#4815][16x][to take-8; conceive-5; help-2; caught]

Note: Sin will take you further than you want to go, keep you longer than you want to stay, make you pay more than you want to pay. Sin will not stop until it destroys you.

> *Sin thrills -* **Heb. 11:25 "the pleasures of sin for a season"**

> *Sin chills -* **Mat. 24:12 "because iniquity shall abound, the love of many shall wax cold"**

> *Sin kills -* **Rom. 6:23 "the wages of sin is death"**

James 1:16 Do not err, my beloved brethren.

Note: "err" [#4105][39x][deceive-24; err-6; gone astray-5; seduce-2; wandered; be out of the way]

The Source of Good Things

James 1:17 Every good gift and every perfect gift is from above, and cometh down from the Father of lights, with whom is no variableness, neither shadow of turning.

Note: Whether answer to prayer or handfuls on purpose, God is the supplier to every good thing that we have.

Note: God does not and will not change.

> **Hebrews 13:8** *Jesus Christ the same yesterday, and to day, and for ever.*

The New Birth Requires the Word of God

James 1:18 Of his own will **begat he us with the word of truth**, that we should be a kind of firstfruits of his creatures.

> *Note: (#616)(2x)(v.15 "bringeth forth" & v.18 "begat")*

> *Note: Salvation only comes through the word of God.*

> **Rom 10:17** *So then **faith cometh by hearing, and hearing by the word of God**.*

> **1Pet 1:23** *Being **born again**, not of corruptible **seed**, but **of incorruptible**, **by the word of God**, which liveth and abideth forever.*

> **Jas 1:21** *Wherefore lay apart all filthiness and superfluity of naughtiness, and receive with meekness **the engrafted word, which is able to save your souls**.*

> **2Tim 3:15** *And that from a child thou hast known **the holy scriptures**, which are **able to make thee wise unto salvation through faith which is in Christ Jesus**.*

Holy Living

James 1:19 Wherefore, my beloved brethren, let every man be swift to hear, slow to speak, slow to wrath:

Note: The less you say, the less you sin.

Prov 17:28 *Even a fool, when he holdeth his peace, is counted wise: and he that shutteth his lips is esteemed a man of understanding.*

Note: One of the things that passage above teaches is that the individual that is quick to speak typically also has a quick temper. The one that is swift to hear will also be a quick learner

Beware of Temper

James 1:20 For the wrath of man worketh not the righteousness of God.

Note: "worketh" [#2716][24x][work-15; do deed; to perform; wrought; causeth; doeth-5]

Note: See the following for warnings of the temper:

> **Proverbs 14:29** *He that is slow to wrath is of great understanding: but he that is hasty of spirit exalteth folly.*

> **Proverbs 15:18** *A wrathful man stirreth up strife: but he that is slow to anger appeaseth strife.*

> **Proverbs 16:32** *He that is slow to anger is better than the mighty; and he that ruleth his spirit than he that taketh a city.*

Proverbs 19:19 *A man of great wrath shall suffer punishment: for if thou deliver him, yet thou must do it again.*

Proverbs 29:22 *An angry man stirreth up strife, and a furious man aboundeth in transgression.*

Note: Anger is not a sin. What we do when angry is what usually gets us in trouble. Staying angry also can get us into serious trouble. Notice the following passage.

(Eph 4:26) *Be ye angry, and sin not: let not the sun go down upon your wrath:*

James 1:21 Wherefore lay apart all filthiness and superfluity of naughtiness, and receive with meekness the engrafted word, which is able to save your souls.

Note: lay apart [#659][8x][laid down; cast off; put off-2; lay aside-2; lay apart; put away]

Note: "superfluity" [#4050][4x][abundance-2; abundantly; superfluity]

Note: "naughtiness" [#2549][11x][evil; wickedness; maliciousness-2; malice-6; naughtiness]

Note: See notes at v. 18 on "the word of God being necessary for salvation".

Dealing with the Word of God
Do Not Just Hear the Word, Believe
it, Do it, and Live by It

James 1:22 But be ye doers of the word, and not hearers only, deceiving your own selves.

James 1:23 For if any be a hearer of the word, and not a doer, he is like unto a man beholding his natural face in a glass:

> *C.R.* **Heb 4:2** *For unto us was the gospel preached, as well as unto them: but the word preached did not profit them,* **_not being mixed with faith in them that heard it._**

> *Just listening to the word of God without doing what it says does not do you any good and it does not change your life. Just listening only has a deceptive affect.*

> **Matt 4:4** *But he answered and said, It is written,* **_Man shall not live by bread alone, but by every word that proceedeth out of the mouth of God_**.

James 1:24 For he beholdeth himself, and goeth his way, and straightway forgetteth what manner of man he was.

> *Note: "straightway" [2112][80x](immediately-35; straightway-32; forthwith-7; misc.-6)*

> *Note: If we are sensitive to the word of God, we will allow it to show us how sinful we really are, otherwise we will forget how bad we really are and how much we need God.*

James 1:25 But whoso looketh into the perfect law of liberty, and continueth [therein], he being not a forgetful hearer, but a doer of the work, this man shall be blessed in his deed.

Note: We miss so many blessings by not following God's instructions.

True Religion versus Vain Religion

James 1:26 If any man among you seem to be religious, and bridleth not his tongue, but deceiveth his own heart, this man's religion [is] vain.

Note: The man that does not control his tongue has a vain religious lifestyle.

Note: Notice the following list showing the different ways the word, "religion" is used in the Bible.

*Note: "religious" [#2357][1x][**James 1:26**]*

*"religion" [#2356][4x][**Acts 26:5; James 1:26-27;** worshipping-**Col. 2:18**]*

*"religion" [#2454][2x]["Jews' religion" **Gal. 1:13-14**]*

"religious" [#4576][10x][religion; worship-6; devout-3]

Note: The less you say, the less you sin. Bridle your Tongue.

James 1:27 Pure religion and undefiled before God and the Father is this, To visit the **<u>fatherless</u>** and widows in their affliction, [and] to keep himself unspotted from the world.

Note: "pure" [#2513][28x][pure-17; clean-10; clear-Rev. 21:18]

*Note: "fatherless" [#3737][2x][John 14:18-**<u>comfortless</u>**]*

Note: "affliction" [#2347][45x][tribulation-21; affliction-17; anguish; trouble-3; persecution; burdened; to be afflicted]

Note: "unspotted" [#784][4x][without spot-I Tim. 6:14 ; I Pet. 1:19 ; II Pet. 3:14]

*(**1Tim 6:14**) That thou keep this commandment **<u>without spot</u>**, unrebukeable, until the appearing of our Lord Jesus Christ:*

*(**1Pet 1:19**) But with the precious blood of Christ, as of a lamb without blemish and **<u>without spot</u>**:*

*(**2Pet 3:14**) Wherefore, beloved, seeing that ye look for such things, be diligent that ye may be found of him in peace, **<u>without spot</u>**, and blameless.*

Note: Pure religion not only makes a person control their tongue, it also causes him to visit the needy and comfortless and also clean up his worldly life. Pure religion can only come from being born again.

(John 3:3) *Jesus answered and said unto him, Verily, verily, I say unto thee,* **<u>Except a man be born again, he cannot see the kingdom</u>** *of God.*

(John 3:5) *Jesus answered, Verily, verily, I say unto thee,* **<u>Except a man be born of water and of the Spirit, he cannot enter into the kingdom of God.</u>**

(John 3:7) *Marvel not that I said unto thee,* **<u>Ye must be born again</u>**.

(John 3:16) For God so loved the world, that he gave his only begotten Son, that whosoever believeth in him should not perish, but have everlasting life.

18

James Chapter 2

Dealing with Prejudice
True Faith has no Respect of Persons

James 2:1 My brethren, have not the faith of our Lord Jesus Christ, [the Lord] of glory, with respect of persons.

Note: "respect of persons" [4382][4x][all the same]

> *[**Rom. 2:11**; **Eph. 6:9**; **Col. 3:25**] all say God is no respect of persons.*

Three areas in our lives have great problems of prejudice in our society today. They are as follows:

1) *Height of stature*
2) *Color of skin*
3) *Geographical location of birth*

We don't have control over any of them but yet some hate others because of their different height, color, or birth location as if they did had control over their own.

Prejudice versus Rich and Poor

James 2:2 For if there come unto your **assembly** a man with a gold ring, in goodly apparel, and there come in also a poor man in vile raiment;

Note: "assembly" [#4864][57x][synagogue-55; congregation; assembly]

James 2:3 And ye have respect to him that weareth the gay clothing, and say unto him, Sit thou here in a good place; and say to the poor, Stand thou there, or sit here under my footstool:

James 2:4 Are ye not then partial in yourselves, and are become judges of evil thoughts?

Faith versus Rich and Poor

James 2:5 Hearken, my beloved brethren, Hath not God chosen the poor of this world rich in faith, and heirs of the kingdom which he hath promised to them that love him?

James 2:6 But ye have **despised** the poor. Do not rich men oppress you, and draw you before the judgment seats?

Note: "despised" [#818][6x][entreated shamefully; do dishonor-3; suffer shame; despise]

Note: The friend that can be bought with money is a very cheap friend.

James 2:7 Do not they **blaspheme** that **worthy** name by the which ye are called?

Note: "blaspheme" [987][35x][blaspheme-17; reviled; railed on-2 ; slanderously reported ; evil spoken of-10 ; defamed; blasphemer; speak blasphemy; blasphemously]

Note: "worthy" [2570][102x][good-83; meet-2; better-7; honest-5; fair; well; misc-3]

The Royal Law

James 2:8 If ye fulfil the royal law according to the scripture, <u>**Thou shalt love thy neighbour as thyself**</u>, ye do well:

Note: "royal" [937][5x][nobleman-2; royal-2; king's]

*Note: C.R. **Lev 19:18** Thou shalt not avenge, nor bear any grudge against the children of thy people, but <u>**thou shalt love thy neighbour as thyself**</u>: I am the LORD.*

[Other verses on "loving one another"]

> **Matt 22:37** *Jesus said unto him, Thou shalt love the Lord thy God with all thy heart, and with all thy soul, and with all thy mind.* **38** *This is the first and great commandment.* **39** *And the second is like unto it,* <u>***Thou shalt love thy neighbour as thyself.***</u> **40**

> On these two commandments hang all the law and the prophets.

> **Mark 12:29** *And Jesus answered him, The first of all the commandments is, Hear, O Israel; The Lord our God is one Lord:* **30** *And thou shalt love the Lord thy God with all thy heart, and with all thy soul, and with all thy mind, and with all thy strength: this is the first commandment.* **31** *And the second is like, namely this,* <u>**Thou shalt love thy neighbour as thyself.**</u> *There is none other commandment greater than these.*

> **John 15:12** *This is my commandment, That ye* <u>**love one another**</u>*, as I have loved you.* **13** *Greater love hath no man than this, that a man lay down his life for his friends.*

> **John 15:17** *These things I command you, that ye* <u>**love one another**</u>*.*

> **Rom 13:8** *Owe no man any thing, but to* <u>**love one another**</u>*: for he that loveth another hath fulfilled the law.* **9** *For this, Thou shalt not commit adultery, Thou shalt not kill, Thou shalt not steal, Thou shalt not bear false witness, Thou shalt not covet; and if there be any other commandment, it is briefly comprehended in this saying, namely,* <u>**Thou shalt love thy neighbour as thyself.**</u> **10** *Love worketh no ill to his neighbour: therefore love is the fulfilling of the law.*

To be a Respect of Persons is Sin

James 2:9 But if ye have respect to persons, ye commit sin, and are **convinced** of the law as transgressors.

Note: "convinced" [1651][17x][tell his fault; reproved-6; convicted; rebuke-5; convince-4]

James 2:10 For whosoever shall keep the whole law, and yet offend in one [point], he is **guilty** of all.

Note: "guilty" [#1777][10x][danger of-5; guilty of-4; subject to]

Note: If we have the ability to break one law, we have the potential to break all laws. The phrase, "guilty of all," is also translated "danger of."

James 2:11 For he that said, Do not commit adultery, said also, Do not **kill**. Now if thou commit no adultery, yet if thou **kill**, thou art become a transgressor of the law.

*Note: "kill" [#5407][12x][kill-10; **Mat. 19:18** - murder; slay]*

*Note: C.R. **Exod 20:13** Thou shalt not kill. **14** Thou shalt not commit adultery.*

***Deut 5:17** Thou shalt not kill. **18** Neither shalt thou commit adultery.*

> ***Mat 19:18*** *He saith unto him, Which? Jesus said,* **_Thou shalt do no murder_**, *Thou shalt not commit adultery, Thou shalt not steal, Thou shalt not bear false witness,*

Note: It needs to be pointed out that not all killing is murder. For example, in self-defense or in capital punishment and when the killing is an accident, none of these are murder.

Judgment by the Word of God

James 2:12 So speak ye, and so do, as they that shall be judged by the **law of liberty**.

> *Note: (We are judged by the law of liberty.)(the word of God)*

> ***Jas 1:25*** *But whoso looketh into the perfect **_law of liberty_**, and continueth therein, he being not a forgetful hearer, but a doer of the work, this man shall be blessed in his deed.*

> ***John 12:48*** *He that rejecteth me, and receiveth not my words, hath one that judgeth him: **_the word that I have spoken, the same shall judge him in the last day._***

Judgment without Mercy

James 2:13 For he shall have judgment without mercy, that hath shewed no mercy; and mercy rejoiceth against judgment.

Note: Judgment without mercy is to receive exactly what we deserve. [Hell forever and ever] No one in their right mind wants to receive what they deserve.

Judgment with mercy is to not receive what we deserve. [Heaven due to salvation and rewards due to service]

Matthew 5:7 *Blessed are the merciful: for they shall obtain mercy.*

Vain Faith versus True Faith
You Can Hear Vain Faith Talk but You
Can Not See Vain Faith Work

James 2:14 What [doth it] **profit**, my brethren, though **a man say** he hath faith, and have not works? can faith save him?

Note: "profit" [#3786][3x][profit-2; advantageth]

Note: "works" [#2041][176x][works-152; deeds-22; labour-1; doing-1]

Note: The faith that does not produce salvation does not produce works.

> *Works are a result of salvation not a requirement for salvation.*

Vain Faith is Just Talk

James 2:15 If a brother or sister be naked, and destitute of daily food,

James 2:16 And **one of you say** unto them, Depart in peace, be [ye] warmed and filled; notwithstanding ye give them not those things which are needful to the body; what [doth it] profit?

Note: See the use of the word "say". The faith that only talks, is a vain faith, and only deceives people into thinking they are saved. Remember, talk is cheap.

Vain Faith Gets No Results

James 2:17 Even so faith, if it hath not works, is dead, being alone.

Note: True faith changes more than your talk. It also changes your walk. Faith is only true when it is put in Jesus Christ and what He did on the cross for salvation.

Man Sees Our Faith Through Our Works

James 2:18 Yea, a man may say, Thou hast faith, and I have works: shew me thy faith without thy works, and **I will shew thee my faith by my works**.

Note: The only way we can see a person's faith is through their works. Man sees our faith by looking at our works, but God sees our faith by simply looking upon the heart.

Vain Faith is General and not
Specifically Believing in Christ

James 2:19 Thou believest that there is one God; thou doest well: the devils also believe, and tremble.

Note: It does not say here that the devils believe the Gospel of Jesus Christ.

It says just that they believe there is one God. Just because you are not an Atheist does not mean that you are saved or born again. Believing that there is one God is a far cry from trusting Christ as your personal Savior.

Vain Faith

James 2:20 But wilt thou know, O vain man, that faith without works is dead?

Note: See the following on "vain faith"

> *1Cor 15:2 By which also ye are saved, if ye keep in memory what I preached unto you, **unless ye have believed in vain**.*

> *1Cor 15:14 And if Christ be not risen, then is our preaching vain, and **your faith is also vain.***

Note: In the passages above, the individuals that were addressed believed in Jesus, but they did not believe in a resurrection. Hence, their faith is vain. Notice the following.

(Rom 10:9) *That if thou shalt confess with thy mouth the Lord Jesus, and* ***shalt believe in thine heart that God hath raised him from the dead, thou shalt be saved.***

Note: There are many that believe in Christ but are actually depending on their lifestyle and the deeds that they do to get them to heaven. Their faith is vain. Notice the following.

(Rom 10:14) ***How then shall they call on him in whom they have not believed****? and how shall they believe in him of whom they have not heard? and how shall they hear without a preacher?*

Note: It does no good to call on Christ to save you if you are depending on something else to save you.

Inward versus Outward Justification
(In Abraham)

James 2:21 Was not Abraham our father **justified by works**, when he had offered Isaac his son upon the altar?

Note: ***Romans 4:2*** *"For if Abraham were justified by works, he hath whereof to glory; but not before God."*

James 2:21 *is outward justification in the sight of man. See notes at verse 24.*

James 2:22 Seest thou how faith wrought with his works, and by works was faith made perfect?

Note: wrought [4903-5x][working with-2; work together; workers together; that helpeth with]

Note: made perfect [5048-24x][make perfect-12; perfect-4; finish-4; fulfilled-2; be perfect; consecrate]

Note: Keep in mind that genuine faith produces works and genuine faith produces salvation, but nowhere does the Bible teach that works produce salvation.

James 2:23 And the scripture was fulfilled which saith, Abraham believed God, and it was **imputed** unto him for righteousness: and he was called the Friend of God.

Note: "imputed" [#3049][41x][think-9; impute-8; reckon-6; count-5; account-4; suppose-2; reason; number; misc -5]

Note: C.R. **Gen 15:6** *And he believed in the LORD; and he counted it to him for righteousness.*

Note: "Friend of God"

2Chr 20:7 *Art not thou our God, who didst drive out the inhabitants of this land before thy people Israel, and gavest it to the seed of* **Abraham thy friend** *for ever?*

Isa 41:8 *But thou, Israel, art my servant, Jacob whom I have chosen, the seed of* **Abraham my friend**.

Note: The salvation of Abraham is mentioned in **Gen. 15:6** *but his work of faith happens later in* **Gen. 22**. *The* *work of faith in Chapter 22 is a result of the saving faith mentioned in Chapter 15.*

Outward Justification

James 2:24 Ye see then how that **by works a man is justified**, and not by faith only.

Note: This is outward justification in the sight of man. There are two types of justification.

The one is justification of the sinner before God which is by faith in Christ alone.

See the following passages of scripture.

> ***Acts 13:39** And by him **all that believe are justified from all things**, from which ye could not be justified by the law of Moses.*

> ***Rom 3:20** Therefore **by the deeds of the law there shall no flesh be justified** in his sight: for by the law is the knowledge of sin.*

> ***Rom 3:24** **Being justified freely by his grace** through the redemption that is in Christ Jesus: **25** Whom God hath set forth to be a propitiation through faith in his blood, to declare his righteousness for the remission of sins that are past, through the forbearance of God; **26** To declare, I say, at this time his righteousness: that he might be just, and **the justifier of him which believeth in Jesus.***

Rom 3:28 Therefore we conclude that **_a man is justified by faith without the deeds of the law._**

Rom 3:30 Seeing it is **_one God, which shall justify the circumcision by faith, and uncircumcision through faith_**.

Rom 4:2 **_For if Abraham were justified by works, he hath whereof to glory; but not before God._**

Rom 5:1 Therefore **_being justified by faith_**, we have peace with God through our Lord Jesus Christ:

Rom 5:9 Much more then, being **_now justified by his blood_**, we shall be saved from wrath through him.

Rom 5:18 Therefore as by the offence of one judgment came upon all men to condemnation; even so by the righteousness of one the **_free gift came upon all men unto justification of life._**

Gal 2:16 Knowing **_that a man is not justified by the works of the law, but by the faith of Jesus Christ, even we have believed in Jesus Christ, that we might be justified by the faith of Christ, and not by the works of the law: for by the works of the law shall no flesh be justified._**

Gal 3:8 And the scripture, foreseeing **_that God would justify the heathen through faith_**, preached before the gospel unto Abraham, saying, In thee shall all nations be blessed.

> **Gal 3:11** <u>**But that no man is justified by the law in the sight of God, it is evident: for, The just shall live by faith**</u>.

> **Gal 3:24** *Wherefore the law was our schoolmaster to bring us unto Christ, that we might be* <u>**justified by faith**</u>.

The other is <u>**outward justification**</u> *which is by works but it is the justification of the believer in the eyes of man as in* **James 2:24-25**. *Notice the following passage concerning outward justification by our works or in this case by our words.*

> **Matt 12:37** *For* <u>**by thy words thou shalt be justified**</u>, *and* <u>**by thy words thou shalt be condemned.**</u>

There is the inward justification is in the eyes of God and the outward justification is in the eyes of man. The seeking to be justified by man is to review the works of man to give evidence of the inward justification. Mankind cannot see your faith, so he must examine your works to see evidence of your faith and to see if the faith is real or not. Faith just like the wind cannot be seen by mankind, but we look for the moving of the trees to reveal the wind and the good deeds and works to reveal the faith. Notice the following verse again.

> **James 2:18** *Yea, a man may say, Thou hast faith, and I have works: shew me thy faith without thy works, and* <u>**I will shew thee my faith by my works**</u>.

Note: Notice the statement that John the Baptist made concerning individuals that approached him for baptism.

(Matt 3:8) Bring forth therefore fruits meet for repentance:

Example of Real Faith and Outward Justification
(In Rahab)

James 2:25 Likewise also was not Rahab the harlot **justified by works**, when she had received the messengers, and had sent [them] out another way?

Vain Faith Compared to a Dead Body
(Both are Empty)

James 2:26 For as the body without the spirit is dead, so faith without works is dead also.

Note: **Titus 1:16** *"They profess that they know God; but in works they deny him, being abominable, and disobedient, and unto every good work reprobate."*

Note: Faith alone saves alone, but the faith that saves is not alone.

Note: True faith produces salvation and true faith produces works but works can never produce salvation.

Titus 3:5 *Not by works of righteousness which we have done, but according to his mercy he saved us, by the washing of regeneration, and renewing of the Holy Ghost;*

Gal 2:16 *Knowing that a man is not justified by the works of the law, but by the faith of Jesus Christ, even we have believed in Jesus Christ, that we might be justified by the faith of Christ, and not by the works of the law: for by the works of the law shall no flesh be justified.*

Eph 2:8 *For by grace are ye saved through faith; and that not of yourselves: it is the gift of God:* **9** *Not of works, lest any man should boast.*

Now notice after **Eph 2:8-9** *the statement that is made is verse* **10**.

Eph 2:10 *For* <u>**we are his workmanship, created in Christ Jesus unto good works**</u>*, which God hath before ordained that we should walk in them.*

Clearly, verse 10 makes us know that works is a result of salvation and not a requirement for salvation.

Just like a body without a soul is dead so faith without works is a dead faith.

19

James Chapter 3

Responsibility
Unto Whom Much is Given, Much is Required

James 3:1 My brethren, be not many masters, knowing that we shall receive the greater condemnation.

Note: "masters" [#1320][58x][doctors-1; teacher-10; masters-47]

Note: "condemnation" [#2917][28x][damnation-7; judgment-13; condemnation-5; be condemned; go to law; avenge]

Luke 12:48 *But he that knew not, and did commit things worthy of stripes, shall be beaten with few stripes. **<u>For unto whomsoever much is given, of him shall be much required</u>**: and to whom men have committed much, of him they will ask the more.*

Dealing with the Tongue

James 3:2 For in many things we offend all. If any man offend not in word, the same [is] a perfect man, [and] able also to bridle the whole body.

Note: "offend" [#4417][5x][offend-3; have stumbled; fall]

Note: If you can get your tongue under control, you can control your whole body. The less you say the less you sin.

Bits and Helms Compared to the Tongue

James 3:3 Behold, we put **bits** in the horses' mouths, that they may obey us; and we turn about their whole body.

James 3:4 Behold also the ships, which though [they be] so great, and [are] driven of fierce winds, yet are they turned about with a very small **helm**, whithersoever the governor listeth.

Note: "helm" [4079][2x][Acts 27:40-rudder]

Note: "governor" [2116][2x][make straight]

Note: "listeth" [1014][34x][will-15; would-11; be minded-2; intend-2; be disposed; be willing; list; of his own will]

The Dangers of the Tongue

James 3:5 Even so the tongue is a little member, and <u>boasteth great things</u>. Behold, how great a matter a little fire kindleth!

Note: The tongue is a little member.

Note: The tongue is a great boaster.

*Note: **Matt. 12:34** & **Luke 6:45** "out of the abundance of the heart the mouth speaketh"*

James 3:6 And the tongue [is] a fire, a world of iniquity: so is the tongue among our members, that it defileth the whole body, and setteth on fire the course of nature; and it is set on fire of hell.

Note: The tongue is a fire.

Note: The tongue is a world of iniquity.

Note: The tongue can defile the whole body.

The Tongue is Uncontrollable by Man

James 3:7 For every kind of beasts, and of birds, and of serpents, and of things in the sea, is tamed, and hath been tamed of mankind:

James 3:8 But the tongue can no man tame; [it is] an unruly evil, full of deadly poison.

Note: The tongue cannot be tamed by man.

Note: The tongue is an unruly evil.

Note: The tongue is full of deadly poison.

The Tongue and Hypocrisy

James 3:9 Therewith bless we God, even the Father; and therewith curse we **men, which are made after the similitude of God.**

> *Note: C.R.* **Gen 1:26** *And God said,* **Let us make man in our image, after our likeness**: *and let them have dominion over the fish of the sea, and over the fowl of the air, and over the cattle, and over all the earth, and over every creeping thing that creepeth upon the earth.* **27** *So* **God created man in his own image, in the image of God created he him**; *male and female created he them.*

James 3:10 Out of the same mouth proceedeth blessing and cursing. My brethren, these things ought not so to be.

Note: Cursing or profanity is forbidden.

> **Colossians 3:8** *But now ye also put off all these; anger, wrath, malice, blasphemy,* **filthy communication out of your mouth**.

> **Matthew 12:36** *But I say unto you, That* **every idle word that men shall speak, they shall give account thereof in the day of judgment**.

Exodus 20:7 *Thou shalt not take the name of the LORD thy God in vain; for the LORD will not hold him guiltless that taketh his name in vain.*

Romans 3:14 *Whose mouth is full of cursing and bitterness:*

Matthew 5:34-37 *But I say unto you, Swear not at all; neither by heaven; for it is God's throne:* ***35*** *Nor by the earth; for it is his footstool: neither by Jerusalem; for it is the city of the great King.* ***36*** *Neither shalt thou swear by thy head, because thou canst not make one hair white or black.* ***37*** *But let your communication be, Yea, yea; Nay, nay: for whatsoever is more than these cometh of evil.*

Proverbs 4:24 *Put away from thee a froward mouth, and perverse lips put far from thee.*

James 3:11 Doth a fountain send forth at the same place sweet [water] and bitter?

James 3:12 Can the fig tree, my brethren, bear olive berries? either a vine, figs? so [can] no fountain both yield salt water and fresh.

The Tongue with Meekness of Wisdom

James 3:13 Who [is] a wise man and endued with knowledge among you? let him shew out of a good conversation *(behavior)* his works with meekness of wisdom.

Note: Meekness is not anxious to get in the first word or have the last word.

*Note: **James 1:19** "be swift to hear, slow to speak, slow to wrath".*

Dealing with Envying and Strife

James 3:14 But if ye have bitter envying and strife in your hearts, glory not, and lie not against the truth.

Earthly Wisdom versus Heavenly Wisdom

James 3:15 This wisdom descendeth not from above, but [is] earthly, sensual, devilish.

Note: "wisdom" [#4678][51x][all translated "wisdom"][4 times in James]

[James 1:5; 3:13, 15, 17]

Note: "descendeth" [#2718][13x][came down-5; come-3; go down-2;departed; descend; had landed]

Note: "earthly" [#1919][7x][earthly-4; terrestrial-2; in earth]

Note: "sensual" [#5591][6x][natural-4; sensual-2]

Note: Wisdom is knowing how to use knowledge. Some use knowledge in a bad way.

James 3:16 For where envying and strife [is], there [is] confusion and every evil work.

Note: Get the point of this passage. If envy and strife is present, so is confusion and every evil work.

Note: "envying" [#2205][17x][zeal-6; envying-5; indignation-2; fervent mind; jealously; emulation; envy]

Note: "strife" [#2052][7x][strife-5; contentious-2]

*[**Prov. 13:10** "only by pride cometh contention"]*

Note: "confusion" [#181][5x][confusion-2; commotions ; tumults-2]

*[**I Cor. 14:33** "God is not the aurthor of confusion, but of peace"]*

Note: "work" #[4229][11x][thing-6; business; matter-3; work]

Heavenly Wisdom

James 3:17 But the wisdom that is from above is first pure, then peaceable, **gentle**, [and] easy to be intreated, full of mercy and good fruits, without partiality, and without hypocrisy.

Note: "gentle" [1933][5x][gentle-3; moderation; patient]

Note: Comparing the two types of wisdom.

I. *The Bad Wisdom*
   *[**Jer. 4:22** "wise to do evil"]*
   *[**Prov. 3:7** wise in thine own eyes]*
   1) *earthly*
   2) *sensual or natural*
   3) *devilish*

II) *The Good Wisdom*
   1) *Pure*
   2) *Peaceable*
   3) *Gentle or patient*
   4) *Submissive*
   5) *Full of mercy and good fruits*
   6) *Impartial*
   7) *Not hypocritical*

James 3:18 And the fruit of righteousness is sown in peace of them that make peace.

*Note: [**Matt. 5:9**] "Blessed are the peacemakers: for they shall be called the children of God."*

20

James Chapter 4

Dealing with Sinful Lust
The Battle in our Flesh, the Source
of Wars and Fighting

James 4:1 From whence [come] **wars** and **fightings** among you? [come they] not hence, [even] of your **lusts** that **war** in your members?

Note: "wars" [#4171][18x][war-12; battle-5; fight]

Note: "fightings" [#3163][4x][fightings-2; strifes ; strivings]

Note: "lusts" [#2237][5x][Luke 8:14-pleasures-3; Titus 3:3-II Pet. 2:13]

   [James 4:1, 3; lusts-2]

*Note: C.R. I Pet. 2:11 "abstain from fleshly lusts, which **war** against the soul"*

*Note: "**war**" [#4754][7x][war-5; goeth a warfare; soldier]*

James 4:2 Ye **lust**, and have not: ye **kill**, and desire to have, and cannot obtain: ye fight and war, <u>yet ye have not, because ye ask not.</u>

Note: "lust" [#1937][16x][desired-8; lust-3; would fain ; coveted-3; fain]

Note: "kill" [5407][12x][kill-10; do murder; slay] [Matt. 19:18-murder]

Note: This passage proves desiring something is not the same as asking God for it. See notes at James 1:7 on asking in prayer. (Please see this author's book on "Prayer.")

Wrong Attitude and Motive in Prayer

James 4:3 Ye ask, and receive not, because ye ask **amiss**, that ye may consume [it] upon your lusts.

Note: "amiss" [#2560][16x][sick-7; diseased-2; amiss; evil-2; grievously; sore; miserably; sick people]

Note: Our requests must match God's will before we can expect an answer. Our reason for the request must be right as well as for what we ask.

1 John 5:14 *And this is the confidence that we have in him, that, if <u>we ask any thing according to his will</u>, he heareth us:*

Friendship with Sin is being an Enemy of God

James 4:4 Ye adulterers and adulteresses, know ye not that the friendship of the world is enmity with God? <u>**whosoever therefore will be a friend of the world is the enemy of God**</u>.

> *1 John 2:15-16 Love not the world, neither the things that are in the world. If any man love the world, the love of the Father is not in him. 16 For all that is in the world, the lust of the flesh, and the lust of the eyes, and the pride of life, is not of the Father, but is of the world.*

> *Note: "enmity" [2189][6x][5 times-enmity ; 1 time-hatred-Gal. 5:20]*

> *Note: Here it talks about not being friends with the world. In **John 3:16** the same Greek word for world appears in "for God so loved the world." **James 4:4** is referring to the world of sin and lusts and pride. See **I John 2:15-16** The world in **John 3:16** is referring to the entire human race. We must hate sin but never hate the sinner.*

The Spirit Lusts to Envy

James 4:5 Do ye think that the scripture saith in vain, The spirit that **dwelleth** in us lusteth to envy?

> *Note: "dwelleth" [#2730][47x][dwell-42; dweller-2; 3 times-inhibiters-Rev. 8:13; 12:12; 17:2]*

Note: "lusteth" [#1971][9x][greatly desire-2; lust; greatly long after; long; long after; longed after; earnestly desiring; desire-I Pet. 2:2]

Note: "The spirit that dwelleth in us lusteth to envy" Like other places, this is a general reference from the Old Testament teachings and not a direct quote of the scriptures from the Old Testament.

*[Example: **Acts 20:35** "It is more blessed to give than to receive."]*

Acts 20:35** I have shewed you all things, how that so labouring ye ought to support the weak, and to remember the words of the Lord Jesus, how he said, **It is more blessed to give than to receive.

Note: You will not find a word for word direct quote of this passage anywhere in the Gospels of the New Testament. However, the general teaching of this statement is found there. Notice the passage below.

A General Reference from Christ that Teaches "It is more blessed to give than to receive"

Luke 14:12** Then said he also to him that bade him, When thou makest a dinner or a supper, call not thy friends, nor thy brethren, neither thy kinsmen, nor thy rich neighbours; lest they also bid thee again, and a recompence be made thee. **13** But when thou makest a feast, call the poor, the maimed, the lame, the blind: **14** And **thou shalt be

blessed; *for they cannot recompense thee: for thou shalt be recompensed at the resurrection of the just.*

A General Reference to Christ's Suffering But not a Direct Quote

Mark 9:12 *And he answered and told them, Elias verily cometh first, and restoreth all things; and **how it is written of the Son of man, that he must suffer many things, and be set at nought***.

Luke 18:31 *Then he took unto him the twelve, and said unto them, Behold, we go up to Jerusalem, and **all things that are written by the prophets concerning the Son of man shall be accomplished.***

A General Reference of Scripture but not a Direct Quote

Luke 21:22 *For these be the days of vengeance, **that all things which are written may be fulfilled.***

General References to Christ's Suffering and Resurrection but not Direct Quotes

Luke 24:46 *And said unto them, **Thus it is written, and thus it behoved Christ to suffer, and to rise from the dead the third day***:

John 18:32 *That the saying of Jesus might be fulfilled, which he spake, signifying what death he should die.*

John 19:28 *After this, Jesus knowing that **all things were now accomplished, that the scripture might be fulfilled,** saith, I thirst.*

John 20:9 *For as yet they knew not **the scripture, that he must rise again from the dead.***

Some general Scripture references that teaches us that "*the spirit that dwelleth in us lusteth to envy.*"

Num 5:14 *And the **spirit** of **jealousy** come upon him, and he be **jealous** of his wife, and she be defiled: or if the **spirit** of **jealousy** come upon him, and he be **jealous** of his wife, and she be not defiled:*

Num 5:30 *Or when the **spirit** of **jealousy** cometh upon him, and he be **jealous** over his wife, and shall set the woman before the LORD, and the priest shall execute upon her all this law.*

(Deut 32:21) *They have moved me to jealousy with that which is not God; they have provoked me to anger with their vanities: and **I will move them to jealousy with those which are not a people**; I will provoke them to anger with a foolish nation.*

(Isa 42:13) *The LORD shall go forth as a mighty man, **he shall stir up jealousy like a man of war:** he shall cry, yea, roar; he shall prevail against his enemies.*

Humility and Grace
Three Access Ways to God's Grace

James 4:6 But he giveth more grace. Wherefore he saith, God resisteth the proud, but **giveth grace unto the humble.**

*Note: C.R. **1Pet 5:5** Likewise, ye younger, submit yourselves unto the elder. Yea, all of you be subject one to another, and be clothed with humility: for **God resisteth the proud, and giveth grace to the humble.***

__Prov 3:34__ Surely he scorneth the scorners: but __he giveth grace unto the lowly__.

Note: "resisteth" [#498][5x][resist-4; opposed]

Note: This is one of the three access ways to God's amazing grace and they must be all used at the same time to get access to God's grace.

1) ***Humility to see the need for Help from God***
1Pet 5:5 *Likewise, ye younger, submit yourselves unto the elder. Yea, all of you be subject one to another, and be clothed with humility: for God resisteth the proud, and* **giveth grace to the humble.**

__Jas 4:6__ But he giveth more grace. Wherefore he saith, God resisteth the proud, but **giveth grace unto the humble.**

2) ***Faith in God Depending on God for Help***
Rom 4:16 *Therefore __it is of faith, that it might be by grace__; to the end the promise might be sure to all the seed;*

not to that only which is of the law, but to that also which is of the faith of Abraham; who is the father of us all,

Rom 5:2 *By whom also <u>we have access by faith into this grace</u> wherein we stand, and rejoice in hope of the glory of God.*

3) **Asking God for Help**
Heb 4:16 *Let us therefore <u>come boldly unto the throne of grace, that we may obtain mercy, and find grace to help in time of need</u>.*

Submit to God then Resist the Devil

James 4:7 Submit yourselves therefore to God. **Resist** the **devil**, and he will flee from you.

Note: "resist" [436][14x][resist-9; withstood; withstand-4]

Note: "devil" [1228][38x][devil-35; slanderers; false accusers-2]

Note: The child of God in a backslidden state is extremely vulnerable to Satan. He cannot withstand Satan if he is not living under obedience to God first.

Drawing nigh to God

James 4:8 Draw nigh to God, and he will draw nigh to you. Cleanse [your] hands, [ye] sinners; and purify [your] hearts, [ye] double minded.

Note: Here we are asked to make the first move. "draw nigh to God, and he will draw nigh to you". He made His first move at Calvary now we must make our move to trust Christ as our Savior and then draw nigh to God.

*Note: "double minded" **Jas 1:8** A double minded man is unstable in all his ways.*

James 4:9 Be afflicted, and mourn, and weep: let your laughter be turned to mourning, and [your] joy to heaviness.

Note: When the Christian is in an afflicted and mournful and weeping state, they are more likely to draw nigh to God than when they are in a laughing and joyful state. In the joyful and laughing state the Christian is more apt to be careless. Even though God wants us to be always joyful in the Lord, He never wants us to be careless. Notice the following passages to prove the point.

*Note: C.R. **(Phil 4:4)** Rejoice in the Lord alway: and again I say, Rejoice.*

*Note: C.R. **2Cor 7:10** For **godly sorrow** worketh repentance to salvation not to be repented of: but the sorrow of the world worketh death.*

James 4:10 Humble yourselves in the sight of the Lord, and he shall lift you up.

Note: "humble" [#5013][14x][humble-6; abase-5; humble one self-2; bring low]

Note: "lift up" [#5312][20x][exalt-14; lift up-6]

Note: See the following verses on having a contrite spirit.

Ps 34:18 <u>**The LORD is nigh unto them that are of a broken heart; and saveth such as be of a contrite spirit.**</u>

Ps 51:17 *The sacrifices of God are a broken spirit:* <u>**a broken and a contrite heart**</u>, *O God, thou wilt not despise.*

Isa 57:15 *For thus saith the high and lofty One that inhabiteth eternity, whose name is Holy; I dwell in the high and holy place,* <u>**with him also that is of a contrite and humble spirit**</u>, *to revive the spirit of the humble, and to revive the heart of the contrite ones.*

Isa 66:2 *For all those things hath mine hand made, and all those things have been, saith the LORD: but* <u>**to this man will I look, even to him that is poor and of a contrite spirit, and trembleth at my word.**</u>

Contrite O.T. [#1792 ; #1793 ; #1794 ; #5223]

[#1792] "contrite" [18x][break-3; break in pieces-3; crush-3; bruise-2; destroy-2; contrite; smite; oppress; beat to pieces; humble]

[#1793] "contrite" [3x][contrite-2; destruction]

[#1794] "contrite" [3x][crouched; broken; contrite]

[#5223] "contrite" [3x][lame-2; contrite]

How we Should Deal with Others
Do Not Speak Evil of your Brethren

James 4:11 Speak not evil one of another, brethren. He that speaketh evil of [his] brother, and judgeth his brother, speaketh evil of the law, and judgeth the law: but if thou judge the law, thou art not a doer of the law, but a judge.

One Lawgiver

James 4:12 There is one lawgiver, who is able to save and to destroy: who art thou that judgest another?

Note: "judgest" [2919][114x][judge-88; determine-7; condemn-5; sue-Mat. 5:40; [ordained; concluded; called in question-2; esteem-2; misc-7]

Dealing with the Future
Do Not Take the Future for Granted

James 4:13 Go to now, ye that say, To day or to morrow we will go into such a city, and continue there a year, and buy and sell, and get gain:

James 4:14 Whereas ye know not what [shall be] on the morrow. For what [is] your life?

It is even a vapour, that appeareth for a little time, and then vanisheth away.

James 4:15 For that ye [ought] to say, <u>**If the Lord will, we shall live, and do this, or that**</u>.

James 4:16 But now ye rejoice in your **boastings:** all such rejoicing is evil.

> *Note: "boastings" [#212][2x][I John 2:16-pride of life]*

> > ***1John 2:16** For all that is in the world, the lust of the flesh, and the lust of the eyes, and the **pride** of life, is not of the Father, but is of the world.*

> *Note: The Greek word for "boastings" is also the same Greek word for "pride" as in the "pride of life" in I John 2:16.*

Sin Defined

James 4:17 Therefore to him that knoweth to do good, and doeth [it] not, to him it is sin.

> *Note:*

> 1) *Sin is the transgression of the law. **I John 3:4***
> 2) *An high look, and a proud heart, and the plowing of the wicked, is sin. **Prov. 21:4***
> 3) *The thought of foolishness is sin. **Prov. 24:9***
> 4) *Whatsoever is not of faith is sin. **Rom. 13:23***
> 5) *To him that knoweth to do good, and doeth it not, to him it is sin. **James 4:17***
> 6) *All unrighteousness is sin. **I John 5:17***

21

James Chapter 5

Dealing with the Rich
Warning to the Rich

James 5:1 Go to now, [ye] rich men, weep and howl for your miseries that shall come upon [you].

Note: Some rich people have a tendency to be independent from God and full of pride.

Note: There are many commands and warnings in the New Testament concerning the rich: [G4147-12 times)(rich-11; be increased with goods) & G4148-3 times)(enrich-2; make rich)]

> ***1Tim 6:9*** *But they that will be rich fall into temptation and a snare, and into many foolish and hurtful lusts, which drown men in destruction and perdition.* ***10 For the love of money is the root of all evil****: which while some coveted after, they have erred from the faith, and pierced themselves through*

247

*with many sorrows. **17** Charge them that are rich in this world, that they **be not highminded**, **nor trust in uncertain riches**, **but in the living God**, who giveth us richly all things to enjoy; **18** That they **do good**, that they **be rich in good works**, **ready to distribute**, **willing to communicate**; **19** Laying up in store for themselves a good foundation against the time to come, that they may **lay hold on eternal life**.*

1) *Be not high minded*
2) *Don't trust in uncertain riches.*
3) *Trust in the living God.*
4) *Do good.*
5) *Be rich in good works*
6) *Be ready to distribute.*
7) *Be willingly to communicate.*
8) *Make sure you are saved.*

The Tendency to Waist when Rich

James 5:2 Your riches are corrupted, and your garments are moth-eaten.

James 5:3 Your gold and silver is cankered; and the rust of them shall be a witness against you, and shall eat your flesh as it were fire. Ye have heaped treasure together for the last days.

Note: We will answer to God for what He gives us that goes to waist and what He gives us that is used for the cause of Christ or abused or misused.

Luke 12:21 *So is he that layeth up treasure for himself, and is not rich toward God.*

The story of the talents in **Matt. 25:14-30:** *Talents are money and money represents opportunity. We are judged on how we handle each opportunity.*

Note: "last days" This phrase appears 5 times in the N.T.

*(Acts 2:17) And it shall come to pass in **the last days**, saith God, I will pour out of my Spirit upon all flesh: and your sons and your daughters shall prophesy, and your young men shall see visions, and your old men shall dream dreams:*

*(2Tim 3:1) This know also, that in **the last days** perilous times shall come.*

*(Heb 1:2) Hath in **these last days** spoken unto us by his Son, whom he hath appointed heir of all things, by whom also he made the worlds;*

*(Jas 5:3) Your gold and silver is cankered; and the rust of them shall be a witness against you, and shall eat your flesh as it were fire. Ye have heaped treasure together for **the last days**.*

*(2Pet 3:3) Knowing this first, that there shall come in **the last days** scoffers, walking after their own lusts,*

The last days in **Jas 5:3** *are referring to the last days of the rich man's life.*

The Tendency to Abuse Wages by the Rich

James 5:4 Behold, the hire of the labourers who have reaped down your fields, which is of you kept back by fraud, crieth: and the cries of them which have reaped are entered into the ears of the Lord of sabaoth.

Note: "sabaoth" [4519][2x][Rom. 9:29][def. armies]

Note: If you are being cheated or abused by your boss in some way, cry out to the Lord of armies for help. (See the following passages.)

(Rom 12:17) Recompense to no man evil for evil. Provide things honest in the sight of all men. (Rom 12:18) If it be possible, as much as lieth in you, live peaceably with all men. (Rom 12:19) Dearly beloved, avenge not yourselves, but rather give place unto wrath: for it is written, **Vengeance is mine; I will repay, saith the Lord. (Rom 12:20) Therefore if thine enemy hunger, feed him; if he thirst, give him drink: for in so doing thou shalt heap coals of fire on his head.** *(Rom 12:21) Be not overcome of evil, but overcome evil with good.*

(Ps 94:1) O LORD God, to whom vengeance belongeth; O God, to whom vengeance belongeth, shew thyself.

The Tendency to be Wanton When Rich

James 5:5 Ye have lived in pleasure on the earth, and been wanton; ye have nourished your hearts, as in a day of slaughter.

Note: "lived in pleasure" [5171][1x][def. indulge in luxury]

Note: "wanton" [4684][2x][I Tim. 5:6-that liveth in pleasure]

Note: "nourished" [5142][8x][fed-4; nourish-3; brought up]

The Tendency of Wickedness from the Rich

James 5:6 Ye have condemned [and] killed the just; [and] he doth not resist you.

Note: Please understand that God is not saying it is a sin to be rich. Many of God's people in the Bible were very rich. Many of the kings of Judah were very rich and also very godly people. God is warning that when rich, what do we do with our riches and what does our riches do to us.

Patience
Patience toward the Second Coming
and God's Patience at Salvation

James 5:7 <u>Be patient</u> therefore, brethren, unto the coming of the Lord. Behold, the husbandman <u>**waiteth**</u> for the precious fruit of the earth, and hath <u>**long patience**</u> for it, until he receive the early and latter rain.

Note: "patient" [#3114][10x][be patient-3; have patience-2; have long patience; bear long; suffereth long; be longsuffering; patiently endured] [longsuffering] [James 5:7-8]

Note: These verses below have "patience" and "wait" together besides James 5:7.

Rom 8:25 *But if we hope for that we see not, then do we <u>with patience wait for it.</u>*

Ps 37:7 *Rest in the LORD, and <u>wait patiently for him</u>: fret not thyself because of him who prospereth in his way, because of the man who bringeth wicked devices to pass.*

Ps 40:1 <u>*I waited patiently for the LORD*</u>; *and he inclined unto me, and heard my cry.*

2Thess 3:5 *And the Lord direct your hearts into the love of God, and into the <u>patient waiting for Christ</u>.*

Note: "precious" [5093][14x][precious-8; most precious-2; more precious; dear; dear; honorable]

Note: There are many commands concerning the coming of our Lord:

    (1) *Be patient [**II Thess. 3:5; James 5:7**]*
    (2) *Occupy [**Luke 19:13**]*
    (3) *Be ready [**Mat. 24:44; Luke 12:40**]*
    (4) *Watch [**Mat. 24:42; 25:13; Mk. 13:33, 35**]*
    (5) *Pray [**Mark 13:33; Luke 21:36**]*

Note: It is because of God's grace and patience with us that we are saved.

James 5:8 Be ye also patient; stablish your hearts: for the coming of the Lord draweth nigh.

Note: Each day that goes by, the rapture is one day closer than it was, and it can occur at any moment.

Patience toward Your Fellow Servants

James 5:9 <u>Grudge not</u> one against another, brethren, lest ye be condemned: behold, the judge standeth before the door.

Note: "grudge" [#4727][6x][sighed; groan-3; with grief; grudge]

Note: C.R. "grudge" **Leviticus 19:18** *Thou shalt not avenge,* **<u>nor bear any grudge</u>** *against the children of thy people, but thou shalt love thy neighbour as thyself: I am the LORD.*

> **1 Peter 4:9** *Use hospitality one to another without grudging.*

Note: The judge stands at the door observing our behavior and could come at any moment.

Patience in Suffering

James 5:10 Take, my brethren, the prophets, who have spoken in the name of the Lord, for an example of **suffering affliction, and of patience**.

Note: "patience" [#3115][14x][longsuffering-12; patience-2]

James 5:11 Behold, we count them happy which endure. Ye have heard of the **patience of Job**, and have seen the end of the Lord; that the Lord is very pitiful *(compassionate)*, and of tender mercy.

*Note: "count happy" [#3106][2x][blessed-**Luke 1:48**]*

*Note: "endure" [5278][17x][endure-11; abide; tarried behind; patient; suffer; take it patiently-2-**I Pet. 2:20**] [**James 1:12 ; 5:11**]*

Note: "patience" [#5281][32x][patience-29; patient continuance; enduring]

Note: "very pitiful" [4184][1x][def. extremely compassionate]

Patience in Speech

James 5:12 But above all things, my brethren, swear not, neither by heaven, neither by the earth, neither by any other oath: but **let your yea be yea; and [your] nay, nay; lest ye fall into condemnation.**

Note: C.R.(Remember the less you say the less you sin.)

*(**Matt 5:33**) Again, ye have heard that it hath been said by them of old time, Thou shalt not forswear thyself, but shalt perform unto the Lord thine oaths: (**Matt 5:34**) But I say unto you, Swear not at all; neither by heaven; for it is God's throne: (**Matt 5:35**) Nor by the earth; for it is his footstool: neither by Jerusalem; for it is the city of*

*the great King. (**Matt 5:36**) Neither shalt thou swear by thy head, because thou canst not make one hair white or black. (**Matt 5:37**) But <u>**let your communication be, Yea, yea; Nay, nay: for whatsoever is more than these cometh of evil.**</u>*

Patience in Suffering with Praying and Singing

James 5:13 Is any among you afflicted? let him pray. Is any merry? let him sing psalms.

Note: "afflicted" [2553][4x][endure hardness; suffer trouble; endure affliction; be afflicted]

Note: "merry" [2114][3x][be of good cheer-2; be merry]

*Note: "sing psalms" [5567][5x][sing-3; sing psalms; making melody-**Eph. 5:19**]*

Patience in Sickness

James 5:14 Is any **sick** among you? let him call for the elders of the church; and let them pray over him, anointing him with oil in the name of the Lord:

Note: "sick" [#770][36x][sick-17; impotent; diseased; weak-16; misc-1]

James 5:15 And the prayer of faith shall save the **sick**, and the Lord shall raise him up; and if he have committed sins, they shall be forgiven him.

Note: "sick" [#2577][3x][wearied; fainted; sick]

There are at least six reasons why we experience sickness.

1) *A test from God such as Job had. [**Job 2:3, 7**]*
2) *Chastisement [**I Cor. 11:30**]*
3) *To mold us. [**II Cor. 12:7-9**]*
4) *The curse of sin. (example: childhood diseases)*
5) *To the glory of God. [**John 9:1-3**]*
6) *Due to our own foolishness. (not exercising or eating right or respecting the weather)*

Patience in Sharing

James 5:16 Confess [your] **faults** one to another, and pray one for another, that ye may be **healed**. The **effectual fervent** prayer of a righteous man availeth much.

Note: "faults" [3900][23x][trespasses-9; offences-7; fall-2; sins-3; fault-2]

Note: "healed" [2390][28x][was made whole-2; heal-26]

Note: "effectual fervent" [1754][21x][work 12, show forth (one's) self 2, wrought be effectual, effectually work, effectual fervent, work effectually in, be might in, to do]

Note: "The effectual fervent prayer of a righteous man availeth much." This makes it clear why we should pray. We have not because we ask not. The most powerful thing you can do as a believer is to ask Almighty God to help. Nothing is more powerful than God.

Patience in Supplication

James 5:17 Elias was a man subject to **like passions** as we are, and he prayed earnestly that it might not rain: and it rained not on the earth by the space of three years and six months.

*Note: "like passions" [#3663][2x][**Acts 14:15**]*

Note: C.R. **1Kgs 17:1** *And Elijah the Tishbite, who was of the inhabitants of Gilead, said unto Ahab, As the LORD God of Israel liveth, before whom I stand, there shall not be dew nor rain these years, but according to my word.*

1 James 5:8 And he prayed again, and the heaven gave rain, and the earth brought forth her fruit.

Note: C.R. **1Kgs 18:1** *And it came to pass after many days, that* **the word of the LORD came to Elijah in the third year, saying, Go, shew thyself unto Ahab; and I will send rain upon the earth.**

> *Note: It is important to note that it was God who told Elijah when to pray for it not to rain and to pray for it to rain. "I (God) will send rain upon the earth."*

Patience with Saints

James 5:19 <u>**Brethren**</u>, if any of you do err from the truth, and one <u>convert</u> him;

Note: "err" #4105 (39x)(deceive 24, err 6, go astray 5, seduce 2, wander 1, be out of the way 1)

Note: "convert" #1994 (39x)(turn-16; be converted-6; return-6; turn about-4; turn again-3; misc-4)

Luke 22:32 *But I have prayed for thee, that thy faith fail not: and when thou art <u>converted</u>, strengthen thy brethren. (Jesus talking to Peter)*

Acts 3:19 *Repent ye therefore, and <u>be converted</u>, that your sins may be blotted out, when the times of refreshing shall come from the presence of the Lord;*

The word, "convert" is commonly confused with the word "repent" which means "change of mind." However, "convert" is to "change how one is used."

Note: The passage in James 5:19 is dealing with believers and not unbelievers.

James 5:20 Let him know, that he which <u>converteth</u> the sinner from the error of his way shall save a soul from death, and shall hide a multitude of sins.

Note: "converteth" #1994 (39x)(turn-16; be converted-6; return-6; turn about-4; turn again-3; misc-4)

Note: "error" [4106][10x][error-7; to deceive; deceit; delusion]

Note: "hide" [2572][8x][covered-5; hide-3]

Note: This applies to converting a backslidden brother back on to the right path.

If God's people would be on the alert to help a wayward brother in Christ, we would save a lot of lives and avoid a lot of sins from being committed. The believer is not just here to reach the lost with the gospel, he is also here to help the wayward brother in Christ to get back on the right path. Notice the following passage.

(Gal 6:1) <u>**Brethren, if a man be overtaken in a fault, ye which are spiritual, restore such an one in the spirit of meekness**</u>; *considering thyself, lest thou also be tempted.*

Printed in the United States
By Bookmasters